Learn Every Day About Social Studies

Edited by Kathy Charner

Learn Every Day
About SOCIAL STUDIES

100 BEST IDEAS from TEACHERS

EDITED BY
Kathy Charner
Illustrated by Deb Johnson

© 2011 Gryphon House, Inc.
Published by Gryphon House, Inc.
10770 Columbia Pike, Suite 201
Silver Spring, MD 20901
800.638.0928; 301.595.9500; 301.595.0051 (fax)

Visit us on the web at www.gryphonhouse.com

Illustrations: Deb Johnson

Cover Photo Credit: ©2010 iStockphoto LP. iStockphoto®, iStock®, iStockaudio®, iStockvideo®, iStockalypse™, Vetta® and CopySpace® are registered trademarks of iStockphoto LP. All other marks are the property of their respective owners. www.istockphoto.com.

LIBRARY OF CONGRESS CATALOGING-IN-PUBLICATION DATA
Learn every day about social studies / [edited by] Kathy Charner.
    p. cm. -- (Learn every day)
ISBN 978-0-87659-363-9 (pbk.)
1. Social sciences--Study and teaching (Early childhood)--Activity programs. 2. Early childhood education--Activity programs. I. Charner, Kathy.
  LB1139.5.S64L43 2011
  372.83--dc22
                            2011011472

BULK PURCHASE
Gryphon House books are available for special premiums and sales promotions as well as for fund-raising use. Special editions or book excerpts also can be created to specification. For details, contact the Director of Marketing at Gryphon House.

DISCLAIMER
Gryphon House, Inc., and the author cannot be held responsible for damage, mishap, or injury incurred during the use of or because of activities in this book. Appropriate and reasonable caution and adult supervision of children involved in activities and corresponding to the age and capability of each child are recommended at all times. Do not leave children unattended at any time. Observe safety and caution at all times.

Table of Contents

Note: The books listed in the Related Children's Books section of each activity may occasionally include books that are only available used or through your local library.

Introduction

You have in your hands a great teacher resource! This book, which is part of the Learn Every Day series, contains 100 activities you can use with children ages 3–6 to help them develop a lifelong love of learning, as well as the knowledge and skills all children need to become successful in kindergarten and beyond. The activities in this book are written by teachers and professionals from the field of early childhood education—educators and professionals who use these activities in their classrooms every day.

The activities in this book are organized by curriculum areas, such as Art, Dramatic Play, Outdoor Play, Social Development, and so on, and within these categories according to their age appropriateness, so activities for children ages three and up come first, then activities for children ages four and up, and finally activities for children ages five and up. Each activity has the following components—learning objectives, a list of related vocabulary words, a list of thematically related books, a list of the materials (if any) you need to complete the activity, and directions for preparation and the activity itself. Also included in each activity is an assessment component to help you observe how well the children are meeting the learning objectives. Given the emphasis on accountability in early childhood education, these assessment strategies are essential.

Several activities also contain teacher-to-teacher tips that provide smart and useful ideas, including how to expand the central idea of an activity in a new way, or where to find the materials necessary to complete a given activity. Some activities also include related fingerplays, poems, or songs that you can sing and chant with the children. Children love singing, dancing, and chanting, actions that reinforce children's understanding of an activity's learning objectives.

This book and each of the other books in the series give early childhood educators 100 great activities that require few materials and little, if any, preparation, and are sure to make learning fun and engaging for children.

Handprints USA

3+

LEARNING OBJECTIVES

The children will:
1. Learn about the shape of the United States of America.
2. Develop their memory skills.

Materials

map of the United
States
large piece of paper
red and blue paint
paintbrushes
smocks

VOCABULARY

home   map   outline   United States

WHAT TO DO

1. Show the children the map of the United States. Explain that this is our country.
2. Explain to the children that people use their hands to help other people, and Americans love to help.
3. Teach the children the following song:

   Across the USA by Susan Oldham Hill
   (Tune: "When Johnny Comes Marching Home")
   We're helping all across the USA today;
   Listen! You can hear Americans as they say:
   We'll lend a hand in our states and towns,
   Helping our neighbors all around.
   We all like helping, lending a hand
   To you!

4. Help the children put on their smocks. Set out the paint and paintbrushes, and paint the children's hands one at a time with the color of their choice. **Note:** Be sure to tell the children not to touch one another while they have paint on their hands.
5. Help the children carefully print their hands on the large piece of paper without smearing the paint.
6. Repeat until all the children have printed their hands. Sing the song and admire the "map" that they created.

ASSESSMENT

To assess the children's learning, consider the following:
- Can the children identify the United States of America?
- Were the children able to remember the song?
- Could the children press their handprints onto the map without smearing?

Susan Oldham Hill, Lakeland, FL

Children's Books

America Is... by Louise
Borden
America the Beautiful
by Katharine Lee Bates
and Neil Waldman
*The Berenstain Bears
Lend a Helping Hand*
by Stan and Jan
Berenstain

Red, White, and Fingerpaint

Materials

8" x 10" outline of the United States
fingerpaint paper
red and blue fingerpaint
metallic silver paint
shallow containers
sponges cut in star shapes
newspaper
smocks
scissors (adult use only)

LEARNING OBJECTIVES

The children will:
1. Learn about the shape of the United States of America.
2. Explore painting.

VOCABULARY

America   country   home   map   paint   shape

WHAT TO DO

1. Show the outline of the United States. Ask the children if they can identify what the shape is. Explain that this shows the shape of the country.
2. Ask the children to put on smocks.
3. Put a small dollop of red fingerpaint and a larger one of blue on their papers. Encourage the children to use their hands to cover the entire paper with the paint, blending only a part of the paint so the red and blue still show.
4. When the paintings are dry, trace the outline of the United States onto each painting and cut it out.
5. Show the children how to dip the sponge stars into the silver paint and press down on their paintings. Encourage the children to keep the stars still while pressing down, so the star shape will be distinct.
   Note: It is fine for children to explore creating their own pictures, or to decorate them in a different way.
6. When dry, place the paintings together in a section of the classroom under a banner that reads "Our United States."

SONG

Sing "You're a Grand Old Flag" with the children as they work.

ASSESSMENT

To assess the children's learning, consider the following:
● Can the children identify the United States by its shape?
● How well did the children manipulate the fingerpaint and star sponges?

Children's Books

A Is for America by G. Gregory Roberts
America Is... by Louise Borden
America the Beautiful by Katharine Lee Bates and Neil Waldman

Susan Oldham Hill, Lakeland, FL

Alaska

LEARNING OBJECTIVES

The children will:
1. Develop their map-reading and globe-reading skills.
2. Learn about Alaska.

Materials

North American
  map
large poster board
  or butcher paper
crayons or colored
  pencils

VOCABULARY

| Alaska | arctic fox | cold | Eskimo | ice |
| igloo | Inuit | polar bear | snow | state |

PREPARATION

● Pin up a large piece of poster board or butcher paper in the classroom or on an outside wall. It should be wide enough so all the children can stand and draw on it at the same time.

WHAT TO DO

1. Read one of the books or a related book and talk about Alaska with the children.
2. Show the children where Alaska is on the map. Point out how far north it is from the continental United States.
3. Ask the children what they think it would be like to live in Alaska. Explain that most people there live in cities and towns. What do the children think about igloos and polar bears?
4. Provide each child with markers, crayons, and colored pencils. Invite them to draw and color something about Alaska on the big paper. Make sure each child has enough space. If the children are not sure what to draw, suggest polar bears, igloos, arctic foxes, glaciers, and so on.
5. After the children finish their drawings, help them sign their names below their work.

ASSESSMENT

To assess the children's learning, consider the following:
● Can the children describe Alaska in some way?
● What Alaska features did the children draw?

Children's Books

Alaska by Shelley Gill and Patrick J. Endres
Alaska ABC Book by Charlene Kreeger and Shannon Cartwright
Alaska's Three Pigs by Arlene Laverde and Mindy Dwyer
Count Alaska's Colors by Shelley Gill and Shannon Cartwright

Shirley Anne Ramaley, Sun City, AZ

Flagmakers

LEARNING OBJECTIVES

The children will:
1. Learn how flags serve as symbols.
2. Develop their small motor skills.

Materials

American flag
white construction
paper
markers and
crayons
pre-cut white stars

VOCABULARY

America   country   flag   pride   stripe   symbol

WHAT TO DO

1. Show the children the US flag and talk with the children about what it is and what it stands for. Ask the children if they can remember places where they have seen flags on display.
2. Ask the children if they have ever seen any other flags. Ask the children what the other flags stand for. Does the children's school have its own flag? Explain that there are many different types of flags.

3. Tell the children they will be making their own flags, as symbols for themselves.
4. Provide each child with a rectangular sheet of paper, and observe as they work on their flags. It is fine if the children try to recreate the US flag.
5. As they work, ask questions about what the colors or shapes on the flags mean to the children.
6. When the children finish their work, put all the flags up together in one part of the classroom. Invite the children to compare the colors and designs on their flags.

SONG

Sing "You're a Grand Old Flag" with the children.

Children's Books

America the Beautiful by Katharine Lee Bates and Neil Waldman
F Is for Flag by Wendy Cheyette Lewison
How Many Days to America?: A Thanksgiving Story by Eve Bunting

ASSESSMENT

To assess the children's learning, consider the following:
- Do the children understand that the US flag is a symbol for America?
- Can the children talk about the designs and pictures on their flags, and how they serve as symbols?

Susan Oldham Hill, Lakeland, FL

House Painters

4+

LEARNING OBJECTIVES

The children will:
1. Learn about what a painter does.
2. Develop their small motor skills.

Materials

smocks or old shirts
brushes (1 per child)
tempera paints in several colors
water bowl
rags
old newspapers
shoeboxes (1 per child)

VOCABULARY

brushes   can   paint   spill

PREPARATION

● Draw the outline of doors and windows on the sides of the shoebox.

WHAT TO DO

1. Talk with the children about the homes they live in. Ask the children if the insides or outsides are painted. Explain that there are professionals called painters who do this work.
2. Show the children the materials, and talk about how artistic painting differs from painting buildings.
3. Distribute the shoeboxes and other materials, and invite the children to begin painting them. Remind the children that they should not paint over the doors and windows. **Note:** Remind the children not to get paint on their clothes.
4. Observe the children as they work. Talk about why they chose to paint the buildings certain colors. Ask the children what colors their own homes are.
5. Give the paint plenty of time to dry. Help the children arrange the buildings along a block. Consider asking the children to describe their buildings. Are they houses or apartments, office buildings, or stores? Consider helping the children write the names of the shops and offices on the buildings.

SONG

Hello, Mr. Painter by Shyamala Shanmugasundaram
(Tune: "Baa Baa Black Sheep")

Hello, Mr. Painter
Have you any paint?
Yes sir, yes sir,
Three cans full.

One for my small house,
One for my tall fence,
One for my old car,
Which I bought for 50 cents.

ASSESSMENT

To assess the children's learning, consider the following:
● Can the children paint the shoebox buildings without painting the doors or windows?
● Can the children name the colors they are using?

Children's Books

Dog's Colorful Day by Emma Dodd
Mouse Paint by Ellen Stoll Walsh
Story Painter: The Life of Jacob Lawrence by John Duggleby

Shyamala Shanmugasundaram, Navi Mumbai, India

Leis

LEARNING OBJECTIVES

The children will:

1. Become familiar with a cultural practice in Hawai'i.
2. Learn how to greet their peers.
3. Develop their small motor skills.

Materials

yarn

tape

silk flowers (easiest if there is a hole in the center of the flower once the stem is removed)

straws

VOCABULARY

aloha	beach	haku lei	Hawai'i
island	lei	state	volcano

PREPARATION

- Cut yarn long enough to go over a child's head for a lei necklace.
- Place tape on ends of yarn so they do not fray.
- Pull the silk flowers off the stems.
- Cut straws.

WHAT TO DO

1. Engage the children in a discussion about the state of Hawai'i. Ask the children to describe what they know about the state.
2. Explain to the children that "aloha" is a traditional greeting in Hawai'i (it also means "goodbye" and "love," depending on inflection), and that people arriving in the state are greeted with leis.
3. Show the materials to the children and explain that they will be making leis for one another.
4. To make leis:
   - Tie a knot on the end of a cut length of yarn.
   - String a silk flower on the yarn.
   - Slip a cut straw piece on the yarn.
   - Alternate by adding flower, straw, flower, straw until the yarn is full, and then knot the two ends of the yarn together.
5. Pair children together and have them take turns putting leis on one another and saying "aloha."

ASSESSMENT

To assess the children's learning, consider the following:

- Can the children say "aloha" to one another? Do they know what "aloha" means?
- Were the children able to put their leis together without help?

Christine Kohler, Ballinger, TX

Children's Books

A Is for Aloha by Uilani Goldsberry

Aloha Is ... by Tammy Paikai

Good Night Hawaii by Adam Gamble

Let's Make a Menu

LEARNING OBJECTIVES

The children will:
1. Learn about the function menus serve in restaurants.
2. Develop their small motor skills.

Materials

sample menus
construction paper
markers, crayons,
    and colored
    pencils
stickers or images
    of food
glue sticks (if
    necessary)

VOCABULARY

food   meal   menu   order   restaurant

PREPARATION

● Copy "Welcome to Our Restaurant" or a similar phrase at the top of the sheets of construction paper.

WHAT TO DO

1. Ask the children about their experiences eating at restaurants in their neighborhood.
2. Ask the children how they chose what they wanted to eat while they were in a restaurant. Talk with the children about menus.
3. Show the children some sample menus, and briefly explain the way they are organized.
4. Set out the materials and invite the children to make their own menus. Ask them what they would want to have on their menu if they ran a restaurant. Ask the children how much they would charge for each item.

ASSESSMENT

To assess the children's learning, consider the following:
● Do the children understand the function that menus serve in a restaurant?
● Were the children able to make basic representations of a menu? Can they explain why they chose to include certain foods and not others?

Children's Books

Froggy Eats Out by Jonathan London
Going to a Restaurant by Melinda Beth Radabaugh
Restaurant Owners by Cecilia Minden and Mary Minden-Zins

Laura Wynkoop, San Dimas, CA

Who Lives in This House?

4+

LEARNING OBJECTIVES

The children will:

1. Use their imaginations to "invent" families who live in houses the children choose.
2. Learn social skills by telling the story of their imaginary families to each other.
3. Develop their small motor skills.

Materials

drawing or construction paper (1 sheet per child)
markers and crayons
cut-out pictures of houses, farms, ranches, igloos, and other homes
child-safe scissors
glue sticks

VOCABULARY

children   family   house   imagine

WHAT TO DO

1. Talk with the children about the homes they live in. Ask them to describe the homes, or to imagine different kinds of homes. Show the children the pictures of different kinds of homes.
2. Invite each child to select one of the pictures.
3. Pass out construction paper.
4. Ask the children to glue their house pictures to the construction paper. Next, tell the children to spend a little time imagining what kind of family might live in this house.
5. Provide markers and crayons, and encourage the children to draw the families they imagine might live in their homes. As they draw, ask the children questions about their families, and encourage the children to think up stories about the families. (Also consider having several pictures of people cut out of magazines that the children can simply glue to their construction paper, if they are having trouble drawing their families.)
6. When the children finish, ask them to name their families and then describe their families to other children in the class.

ASSESSMENT

To assess the children's learning, consider the following:
- Were the children able to imagine rich story worlds about their families?
- How well were the children able to glue and draw their family home scenes?

Children's Books

Homes for Everyone by Jennifer B. Gillis
Homes in Many Cultures by Heather Adamson
Mountain Homes by Nicola Barber

Donna Alice Patton, Hillsboro, Ohio

Neighborhood People Portraits

Materials

small picture frames
paper for painting
   cut to fit inside
   the frames
fine black
   permanent
   markers
watercolor paints
paintbrushes

LEARNING OBJECTIVES

The children will:
1. Express thoughts, ideas, and feelings through drawing and painting.
2. Learn to work independently.
3. Show interest in and acknowledge achievements of others.

VOCABULARY

exhibition   frame   neighborhood   painting   portrait

PREPARATION

- Each child could bring along their own inexpensive frame.
- Prepare paper for painting that will match the frame sizes.

WHAT TO DO

1. Talk with the children about people in their neighborhood.
2. Distribute the black markers to the children and ask them to draw someone who is special to them. Have them also draw people in their neighborhoods.

3. Show the children how to use the paint as a "wash" over the black ink drawing portraits.
4. Once dry, insert the pictures into the photo frames and display them around the room as an art exhibition.

TEACHER-TO-TEACHER TIP

- Invite families and people in the children's neighborhoods to attend the art exhibition.

Children's Books

All Families Are Special
by Norma Simon
All Kinds of Families by
Mary Ann Hoberman
The Family Tree by
Todd Parr

ASSESSMENT

To assess the children's learning, consider the following:
- Can the children share their ideas and knowledge with others?
- Do the children express themselves through forms of art?
- Can the children successfully complete the activity, working independently?

Anne Houghton, Melbourne, Victoria, Australia

We Can Build It

5+

LEARNING OBJECTIVES

The children will:
1. Learn about how roads are built.
2. Work together on a project.
3. Explore the use of tape measures and rulers.

Materials

blocks
rulers
tape measures
construction hats
construction
    vehicles
construction cones
paper and markers

VOCABULARY

build   cone   construction site   intersection   measure   road

WHAT TO DO

1. Talk with the children about how they got to class that day. Did they ride on roads? Explain that construction workers build roads to help people get from place to place.
2. Ask the children if they have ever seen construction workers building or improving a road. Ask them what the construction site looked like.
3. Show the children the various materials, and invite them to work together to use the blocks to build a road from one part of the classroom to another. Encourage the children to use the rulers and tape measures to determine the length of the road they will build.
4. After the children finish building one road, consider challenging them to build an additional road that crosses the first road.

TEACHER-TO-TEACHER TIP

- If you can take your children to a construction site for a field trip, this will really inspire them with their building.

ASSESSMENT

To assess the children's learning, consider the following:
- Can the children explain the importance of roads, and how they serve a community?
- Are the children able to work together to construct roads in the classroom?

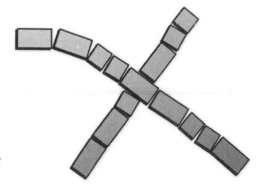

Holly Dzierzanowski, Brenham, TX

Children's Books

Let's Build a Clubhouse by Marilyn Singer
Pooh Builds a House by A.A. Milne
Working Hard with the Mighty Dump Truck by Justine Korman

What Is an Architect?

5+

LEARNING OBJECTIVES

The children will:

1. Become familiar with the word "architect" and its meaning.
2. Make basic blueprints for simple structures.
3. Develop their small motor skills.

Materials

blueprints
pictures of different
 types of buildings
 or structures
rulers
paper
markers and
 crayons
blocks

VOCABULARY

architect   blueprints   building blocks   construction   design   model

WHAT TO DO

1. Gather the children together and ask them if they have heard the term "architect" before. Ask the children to explain what an architect does, or explain the term to them.
2. Show the children the sample blueprints and explain that architects make designs for buildings and then oversee the construction.
3. Put the blueprints in the block center, along with markers, crayons, rulers, and blank paper. Invite the children to practice making sample blueprints, and then to try and build the structures they made blueprints for by using the blocks available in the center.

TEACHER-TO-TEACHER TIP

- Consider inviting an architect to the classroom to talk to the children, and have the architect bring some pictures of the buildings that she helped build.

ASSESSMENT

To assess the children's learning, consider the following:

- Do the children understand what an architect does?
- Are the children able to make simple blueprint designs in the block center?
- How well are the children able to use the blocks to construct the designs they made blueprints for?

Holly Dzierzanowski, Brenham, TX

Children's Books

Architect of the Moon
by Tim Wynne-Jones
Iggy Peck, Architect by
Andrea Beaty
Jack the Builder by
Stuart J. Murphy

The Corner Store

3+

LEARNING OBJECTIVES

The children will:
1. Learn about the function of grocery stores.
2. Learn to identify various items from a grocery store.
3. Role-play purchasing and selling grocery items.

Materials

Supermarket by
   Kathleen Krull
   and Melanie
   Hope Greenberg
toy cash register
   with play money
real coupons for
   food and grocery
   items
hats and purses
shopping baskets
   and carts
play or real, non-
   perishable,
   grocery items
paper grocery bags

VOCABULARY

aisle	cash register	check-out stand	coupons
grocery bag	grocery store	meat	paper towels
shopping cart	supermarket	vegetables	

PREPARATION

● Set up a corner store in the classroom so it resembles a real grocery store.

WHAT TO DO

1. Read *Supermarket* by Kathleen Krull and Melanie Hope Greenberg with the children. Discuss the story with the children. Talk about the importance of grocery stores, and how all communities have them.
2. Point out the corner store set up in the classroom. Invite the children to explore the store and role-play the various positions in the store, from customer to cashier.

TEACHER-TO-TEACHER TIP

● Ask local grocery stores if they will allow you to take a "behind the scenes" field trip to their store. The children will enjoy seeing where trucks are unloaded and where the food is stored before it is displayed.

SONG

The Grocery Store by Jackie Wright
(Tune: "Here We Go 'Round the Mulberry Bush")
This is the way we buy our food,
Buy our food, buy our food.
This is the way we buy our food
In the corner grocery store.

ASSESSMENT

To assess the children's learning, consider the following:
● Do the children understand the importance a local grocery store has for the community?
● Can the children correctly identify various foods or items in the grocery store?

Children's Books

General Store by
   Rachel Field
Grandpa's Corner Store
   by DyAnne DiSalvo
Supermarket by
   Kathleen Krull and
   Melanie Hope
   Greenberg

Jackie Wright, Enid, OK

Stop and Go

3+

LEARNING OBJECTIVES

The children will:

1. Engage in active play using large motor skills.
2. Recognize the reasons for rules.
3. Understand that pictures and symbols have meaning and that print carries a message.

Materials

Red Light, Green Light by Anastasia Suen
green sign
red sign

VOCABULARY

go   green   red   stop

PREPARATION

● Make a pair of red and green signs to resemble stoplights.

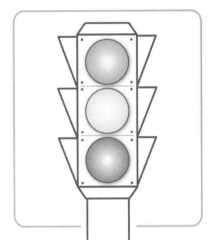

WHAT TO DO

1. Gather the children together and read *Red Light, Green Light* by Anastasia Suen.
2. After reading the book, talk with the children about what happens in the book. Explain why it is important for everyone to follow traffic rules.
3. Show the children the red and green signs, and hand out the various pictures to the children.
4. Have the children line up on all four sides of the room. Using the red and green signs, have the children move safely across the room. Tell them they have to pass those children going in the opposite direction on the right-hand side.
5. After the children understand the basic principle of the activity, select a child to use the red and green signs to direct traffic. Discourage the children from having accidents.

ASSESSMENT

To assess the children's learning, consider the following:

● Can the children identify the colors on the signs and explain what they mean in a traffic situation?
● Can the children obey the traffic signals and take turns passing one another safely from one side of the room to the other?

Children's Books

Green Light for the Little Red Train by Benedict Blathwayt
Red Light, Green Light by Margaret Wise Brown
Red Light Stop, Green Light Go by Andrew Kulman

Carol Hupp, Farmersville, IL

We Are the Same, We Are Different

3+

Materials

scissors (adult use only)

pieces of paper that match various human skin colors

yarn

pieces of paper in a variety of colors (blue, red, yellow, and so on)

globe and/or a world map

Whoever You Are by Mem Fox

glue

markers and crayons

Children's Books

Hats Hats Hats by Ann Morris

Houses and Homes by Ann Morris

Maps and Globes by Jack Knowlton

LEARNING OBJECTIVES

The children will:
1. Learn about maps and/or globes.
2. Learn there are many countries and places in the world.
3. Develop their small motor skills.

VOCABULARY

alike   different   Earth   globe   same   world

PREPARATION

- Cut several different people out of paper that matches human skin colors.
- Cut hair from yarn.
- Cut simple shirts, blouses, pants, and dresses from the colored paper for the dolls to wear.
- Be sure there are several uncut sheets of paper for children to glue the dolls onto.

WHAT TO DO

1. Show the children the globe or a world map. Ask the children if they can identify what it is. Explain that this object represents Earth and that all kinds of people live on Earth.
2. Read the story *Whoever You Are* by Mem Fox.
3. After reading the story, discuss it with the children. Talk about how they are alike and how they are different from each other.
4. Set out the paper cutouts of people, along with the paper clothes, the hair, and the glue.
5. Invite the children to choose a few different paper dolls and glue them to a sheet of paper. Then encourage the children to glue on hair and clothes. Provide markers and crayons so the children can draw faces on their people.
6. Ask the children about the people in their pictures. Are they all alike? Do they look or dress differently? What parts of the world are they from?

ASSESSMENT

To assess the children's learning, consider the following:
- Can the children identify a map or globe and explain what it represents?
- Can the children glue pictures of different people to a sheet of paper?
- Can the children explain where the people in their pictures come from?

Carol Hupp. Farmersville, IL

City Gardens

4+

LEARNING OBJECTIVES

The children will:
1. Learn about growing gardens in the city.
2. Improve their small motor skills.
3. Develop an understanding of planting.
4. Develop their hand-eye coordination.

Materials

small foam cups
herb seedlings for
    each child (Note:
    ensure these are
    all child-safe and
    edible)
soil for planting
old newspapers to
    cover the work
    tables

VOCABULARY

| city | earth | fertilizer | garden | herb |
| plant | season | seed | soil | sprout |

WHAT TO DO

1. Gather the children together and read a book about gardening.
2. Talk with the children about growing plants and flowers in the city. Ask the children if they have ever seen a beautiful flower growing in a city. Talk about how people do not need to live on a farm to have a garden.
3. Show the children the materials and explain the day's project.
4. Encourage the children to talk about plants or gardens at their own homes. Explain how and when to water their plants.
5. Help each child fill a foam cup with soil, put a seedling in the soil, then cover up the root. Help the children write their names on the cups.
6. Set the cups out where they can receive natural light. Encourage the children to check on their plants every few days, to see how they are growing.
7. Help the children water the plants when the soil gets dry.
8. When the plants are well grown, invite the children to take the plants home and replant them in a more permanent location.

ASSESSMENT

To assess the children's learning, consider the following:
- Do the children understand it is possible to grow plants in a city?
- Were the children able to plant and grow their seedlings?

Shirley Anne Ramaley, Sun City, AZ

Children's Books

A Backyard Flower Garden for Kids by Amie Jane Leavitt
Grandma's Garden by Mercer Mayer
Roots, Shoots, Buckets & Boots: Gardening Together with Children by Sharon Lovejoy

Homes Around the World 4+

LEARNING OBJECTIVES

The children will:

1. Explore different kinds of homes around the world.
2. Develop their small motor skills.
3. Improve their language skills.

Materials

construction paper
child-safe scissors
stapler (adult use
    only)
paste or glue
pencils
magazines

VOCABULARY

cabin	city	country	different	home
hut	igloo	teepee	world	

PREPARATION

- Fold a sheet of 8" x 10" construction paper in half. Place two folded sheets of paper inside, and staple them together, making a book. Prepare one book for each child.
- Consider cutting out some pictures ahead of time for children who may have difficulty cutting.

WHAT TO DO

1. Gather the children together and talk about homes. Ask the children to describe their homes, and talk about other kinds of homes they can think of.
2. Read the children a book about different kinds of homes (see Vocabulary list above). Ask the children if any of them have been to homes in other countries, or seen homes different from their own. In the Southwest, for example, many children may have seen Navajo hogans.
3. Set out the materials and invite the children to cut and paste pictures of homes into their own books. Help them as needed.
4. On the front covers of the children's books, help them write, "Homes Around the World" by _____, and sign their names.

ASSESSMENT

To assess the children's learning, consider the following:

- Can the children name different kinds of homes that people live in?
- Were the children able to cut out and paste pictures with minimal help?

Children's Books

City Homes by Nicola Barber
Homes Around the World by Max Moore
Homes on the Water by Nicola Barber
Houses and Homes by Ann Morris and Ken Heyman
Wonderful Houses Around the World by Yoshio Komatsu, Akira Nishiyama, and Naoko Amemiya

Shirley Anne Ramaley, Sun City, AZ

New Neighbors

4+

LEARNING OBJECTIVES

The children will:
1. Develop their patterning and ordering skills.
2. Develop their listening and recall skills.
3. Learn the names of various animals.

Materials

Loudmouth George and the New Neighbors by Nancy Carlson picture-word cards of all the animals in the book

VOCABULARY

after   before   dog   neighbor   pig   rabbit

WHAT TO DO

1. With the children, read the book *Loudmouth George and the New Neighbors* by Nancy Carlson several times to familiarize the children with the sequence of events.
2. Talk with the children about the neighbors that appear in the book. Ask the children what sounds the neighbors make.
3. Mix up the order of the cards and show them to the children.
4. Re-read the story to the children, and invite them to pick up the correct card at the various parts of the story.
5. After finishing the story, challenge the children to recall the order in which the animals appear in the book. Have them work together to place the animal cards in the correct order, identifying the animals as they go.

TEACHER-TO-TEACHER TIP
● Set a copy of the book out for the children to explore.

ASSESSMENT
To assess the children's learning, consider the following:
● Can the children name the animals in the story and on the cards?
● Can the children put the cards in the correct order, based on their memory of the story's sequence of events?

Susan Oldham Hill, Lakeland, FL

Children's Books

Everybody Brings Noodles by Norah Dooley
Noisy Neighbors by Marcia Leonard
Too Much Noise by Ann McGovern

Where? Where? It's on the Map!

LEARNING OBJECTIVES

The children will:
1. Begin to think about geography and mapping.
2. Participate in the visual arts.

Materials

large piece of paper
markers
As the Crow Flies
   by Gail Hartman
pictures of objects
   on the children's
   playground
glue or tape

VOCABULARY

across from	far	houses	maps
near	next to	roads	streets

PREPARATION

● Draw a basic outline of the children's playground on a large sheet of paper, leaving blank spaces where playground equipment belongs.

WHAT TO DO

1. Gather the children together. Read *As the Crow Flies* by Gail Hartman to the children.
2. After finishing the story, engage the children in a discussion about the different creatures in the story, and look at the maps for each section. Point out how at the end of the story, the little maps become part of a big map.
3. Show the children the large prepared map outline. Tell the children they are going to make a map of their own playground.
4. Show the children pictures of the various pieces of playground equipment and challenge the children to indicate where on the maps the equipment belongs.
5. Write the name of the piece of equipment in the blank space on the map, and continue until the map is complete.

ASSESSMENT

To assess the children's learning, consider the following:
● Can the children identify the names of the pieces of equipment on their playground?
● Can the children correctly indicate where the various pieces of playground equipment belong on the map?

Children's Books

Maps and Globes by Jack Knowlton
Me on the Map by Joan Sweeney
There's a Map on My Lap by Tish Rabe

Carol Hupp, Farmersville, IL

You Are My Country

4+

LEARNING OBJECTIVES

The children will:
1. Develop their sense of community pride.
2. Develop their memory skills.
3. Sing a song about America.

Materials

America the Beautiful by Katharine Lee Bates and Neil Waldman
American flag
chart with words to the song

VOCABULARY

America   community   country   flag   home   pride

WHAT TO DO

1. Read the children *America the Beautiful* by Katharine Lee Bates and Neil Waldman. After reading the book, discuss with the children the beautiful places in America that the book mentions.

2. Show the children an American flag and talk with the children about what the symbol means. Explain that the children live in a community, and that everyone in that community needs to respect one another, which means loving and respecting the community.

3. Sing the following song with the children:

You Are My Country by Susan Oldham Hill
(Tune: "You Are My Sunshine")
You are America,
You are my country;
Where I live and where I belong.
I love your cities; I love your hillsides:
And that's why I am singing this song.

I see your flag fly against the white clouds;
I see the stars shine against the blue;
You are America,
You are my country.
And I'm singing this song out to you.

ASSESSMENT

To assess the children's learning, consider the following:
- Can the children explain generally what a community is and why it is important?
- Can the children sing the song?

Susan Oldham Hill, Lakeland. FL

Children's Books

America the Beautiful by Katharine Lee Bates and Neil Waldman
F Is for Flag by Wendy Cheyette Lewison
How Many Days to America?: A Thanksgiving Story by Eve Bunting
State-by-State Guide (United States of America) by Millie Miller

The Land of Australia

5+

LEARNING OBJECTIVES

The children will:
1. Learn about Australia.
2. Develop their vocabularies.
3. Learn about maps and globes.

Materials

books about
  Australia
globe and/or large
  map of the world
pictures of
  kangaroos and
  other unique
  Australian
  animals

VOCABULARY

Australia	country	kangaroo	koala
land	outback	walkabout	wombat

PREPARATION

- Ask teachers, parents, family members, and caregivers if they have been to Australia. Consider sending a note home with the children, or post a message on a board for adults to read. If anyone responds, ask if that person will come to the class and talk about Australia.

WHAT TO DO

1. Read one or more books about Australia with the children (see list to the left).
2. After reading the books, engage the children in a discussion about Australia. Talk about the country's unique animals, including the kangaroo. Show the children pictures of Australian animals, and challenge the children to identify them.
3. Explain that many of the animals are different in Australia because it is an isolated country. Ask the children if they have ever seen a kangaroo at the zoo.
4. Show the children where Australia is on the map or globe. Talk with the children about Australia's distance from the United States, as well as its distance from other countries.

ASSESSMENT

To assess the children's learning, consider the following:

- Can the children name various animals native to Australia?
- Can the children identify Australia on a map or globe?
- Can the children say what letter the word "Australia" begins and ends with?

Shirley Anne Ramaley, Sun City, AZ

Children's Books

Australia by David Petersen
Australia ABCs: A Book About the People and Places of Australia by Sarah Heiman and Arturo Avila
This Is Australia by Miroslav Sasek
Welcome to the World of Kangaroos by Diane Swanson
What Do Kangaroos Do? by Dee Phillips

Look at My City!

5+

LEARNING OBJECTIVES

The children will:
1. Become familiar with the concept of a city.
2. Learn about their particular hometown or city.
3. Develop their small motor skills.

Materials

books about cities (see the Children's Books list for suggestions)

2 pieces of construction paper per student

crayons, markers, art supplies

glue sticks

child-safe scissors

stapler (adult use only)

images of places and things that are specific to the local town or city, including a map

VOCABULARY

capital   city   map   state

WHAT TO DO

1. Read the children a simple book about cities. Talk with the children about some characteristics of cities. If the children live in a city, ask them to describe it. If they do not live in a city, ask the children to describe a city they have visited or know about.
2. Show the children the materials. Tell the children they will be making a small book about their city or town. (**Note:** If the children do not live in a city or town, make the books about a nearby town or city.)
3. To make a City Book, help each child do the following:
   - Fold each piece of construction paper in half. Staple together. Each piece of paper will yield four pages.
   - Glue a picture of the local city map on one page.
   - Draw or cut out pictures that symbolize life in their city.
   - Add stickers, drawings, or cut-out pictures of birds, flowers, city flag, and so on.
   - Have the children draw the cover with their name on it, such as "Joan's City."
4. Help the children with each part of the process if necessary. Observe the children as they work, and engage them in discussions about their books.
5. After the children finish making their books, they can take them home or put them in the class library.

ASSESSMENT

To assess the children's learning, consider the following:
- Can the children name some facts about their city?
- Were the children able to decorate their city books without difficulty?

Donna Alice Patton, Hillsboro, OH

Children's Books

The Little Man in the Map by Andrew Martonyi

My Neighborhood: Places and Faces by Lisa Bullard

State Capitals by Tracy Maurer

Doctor or Veterinarian

4+

LEARNING OBJECTIVES

The children will:

1. Develop language and math skills.
2. Become more informed about doctors and veterinarians.

Materials

card stock or large
  chart paper
picture of a doctor
picture of a
  veterinarian
marker
stickers or self-
  adhesive notes

VOCABULARY

animal	appointment	doctor	examination
hospital	patient	veterinarian	

PREPARATION

- Make a chart by drawing two columns on the card stock or chart paper. In one column, write "doctor" and put a picture of a doctor. In the other column, write "veterinarian" and put a picture of a veterinarian.

WHAT TO DO

1. Gather the children together and ask them if they have ever been to the doctor. Encourage the children to describe their experiences at the doctor's office.
2. Ask the children if they are familiar with the word "veterinarian." Point out that veterinarians are doctors for animals.
3. Ask the children whether they would rather be a doctor or veterinarian when they grow up. Show the children the chart, and have the children take turns putting a sticker or self-adhesive note on one side or the other, indicating what they would rather be when they grow up.
4. Review the children's responses as a group, counting the total number in each column. Talk with the children about why they chose one profession over the other.

ASSESSMENT

To assess the children's learning, consider the following:

- Can the children describe what a doctor and a veterinarian do?
- Can the children indicate which profession they would rather pursue when they grow up?
- Are the children able to determine which profession is more popular in the class?

Jackie Wright, Enid, OK

Children's Books

Daisy the Doctor by
Jo Litchfield and
Felicity Brooks
Going to the Doctor by
Anne Civardi
Sally Goes to the Vet by
Stephen Huneck

Please Send Those Postcards

Materials

map of the United States or a map of the world
small adhesive labels

LEARNING OBJECTIVES

The children will:
1. Listen to the postcards and discuss them.
2. Participate in finding and marking the location on a map.

VOCABULARY

city	country	location	map
postcard	state	United States	world

PREPARATION

- Display the map on a large wall. Mark your location.
- Write a letter requesting postcards from the places the children's parents, family members, and grandparents travel.

WHAT TO DO

1. At the beginning of the school year, send a letter home with the children requesting postcards. (See "Preparation").
2. As the postcards come in, read them to the children and put a number on the postcard, using a label.
3. Mark the location on the map with the same number.
4. Display the cards around the map.
5. Discuss the various places with the children.

ASSESSMENT

To assess the children's learning, consider the following:
- Can the children locate their hometown or city on a map?
- Can the children match the number on the postcard to the location?

Children's Books

My First Book About (Choice of State) series by Carole Marsh
The United States ABC's: a Book About the People and Places of the United States by Holly Schroeder and Jeff Yesh
Babar's USA by Laurent de Brunhoff

Carol Zook, Fort Wayne, IN

The Same All Over

5+

The children will:
1. Identify specific buildings from their neighborhood.
2. Identify similar buildings from other cities.
3. Begin to understand that neighborhoods all over the world have similar needs.

Materials

pictures of school and nearby homes, apartment buildings, stores, schools, firehouse, police station, and so on

pictures of similar buildings from other communities

VOCABULARY

apartment	city	country	firehouse	house
library	neighborhood	police station	school	store

WHAT TO DO

1. Talk with the children about the buildings they see every day. Show the children the pictures from their neighborhood. Ask the children to describe what they see. As the children discuss the pictures, help them make the connection that different types of buildings (houses and apartment buildings) can have the same function.

2. Show the children the pictures of similar buildings in other communities. Challenge the children to identify and describe how the buildings in which people live, shop, and go to school are the same and how they are different. Help the children see that communities across the country and world are alike in many ways because people have similar needs.

TEACHER-TO-TEACHER TIP

• Discuss with the children why buildings in other places look different from those in their community.

Children's Books

Grandpa's Corner Store by DyAnne DiSalvo

My Neighborhood: Faces and Places by Lisa Bullard

My New Town by Kirsten Hall

ASSESSMENT

To assess the children's learning, consider the following:
• Can the children identify buildings in their neighborhood?
• Can the children recognize similar buildings from other communities?
• Can the children suggest certain services that all people need?

Sue Bradford Edwards, Florissant, MO

The Shapes and Colors of Flags

5+

Materials

pictures of flags of several countries (1 per child)
world map

LEARNING OBJECTIVES

The children will:
1. Learn about flags of different countries.
2. Explore shapes, colors, and patterns.

VOCABULARY

design   different   flags   same   shapes

WHAT TO DO

1. Assign a flag to each child, and ask the children to sit in a circle with their flags.
2. Begin by talking with the children about flags and what they represent.
3. Identify the countries associated with the flags each child is holding. Show the children that country on a world map, and mention a few facts about the country.
4. Name a color. Ask all the children who have that color on their flags to raise it above their heads.
5. Repeat this with various colors.
6. Continue the activity by naming different shapes, such as circles, rectangles, squares, and triangles, and having the children wave their flags if they contain those shapes.

TEACHER-TO-TEACHER TIP

● To make the flags more personal for the children, consider giving each child an image of a different flag the day before the activity and asking the children's families to help the children draw copies of the flags on 8″ x 10″ sheets of construction paper to bring in the following day. Or else consider working with the children to create hand-made copies of their flags prior to doing the activity.

ASSESSMENT

To assess the children's learning, consider the following:
● Can the children identify the colors on their flags?
● Can the children identify various shapes on their flags?
● Do the children know the names of the countries associated with their flags?

Children's Books

A Color of His Own by Leo Lionni
F Is for Flag by Wendy Cheyette Lewison
The Shape of Me and Other Stuff by Dr. Seuss

Shyamala Shanmugasundaram, Navi Mumbai, India

Trevor the Traveling Tortoise

LEARNING OBJECTIVES

The children will:
1. Identify their state on a map.
2. Learn about the locations of the various states.

Materials

bulletin board
US map
turtle puppet
small turtle pictures
  or stickers (1 per
  state)

VOCABULARY

country   map   states   travel

PREPARATION

- Hang the US map on the bulletin board.

WHAT TO DO

1. Introduce the children to the turtle puppet, calling him Trevor the Traveling Tortoise. Explain that Trevor lives in the same state as the children, but likes to travel, because his home is on his back.
2. Using Trevor, show the children the location of their state on the map.
3. Attach a small picture of Trevor to the state.
4. Invite one child forward to put on the puppet, playing Trevor.
5. With the rest of the children in the class, ask, "Trevor, where are you traveling today?"
6. Invite Trevor to point to a state on the map and say, "I'm traveling to _____."
7. Give the child playing Trevor a sticker to attach to that state. Invite Trevor and the other children to chant the state's name while Trevor attaches the sticker.
8. Repeat the activity each morning, allowing a different child to choose a state to mark on the US map.

TEACHER-TO-TEACHER TIPS

- Make a quick and easy turtle puppet by pasting a turtle picture to card stock and then attaching it to a tongue depressor.
- Use any puppet in place of a turtle and give the puppet a different name.

Children's Books

Maps and Globes by
Jack Knowlton
North America by
D.V. Georges
When Daddy Travels by
Harriet Ziefert

ASSESSMENT

To assess the children's learning, consider the following:
- Can the children identify their state on the map?
- Can the children say the names of other states, or identify them on the map?

Mary J. Murray, Mazomanie, WI

Put the Fire OUT!

3+

LEARNING OBJECTIVES

The children will:
1. Learn about the job of firefighters.
2. Work together imaginatively.

Materials

garden hose
scissors (adult use only)
red construction paper
firefighter costumes

VOCABULARY

emergency	firefighter	firehouse	hose
hydrant	ladder	pole	siren

PREPARATIONS

- Rinse out the garden hose.
- Allow time for the hose to dry out completely, and then cut the hose into 24"–36" sections.
- Create a picture and word label for the box or storage container for the hose sections.
- Cut out several different-sized fire patterns from the paper.

WHAT TO DO

1. Talk with the children about fire and fire safety. Ask the children if they have ever seen a fire truck in use. Have they seen fire hoses being used?
2. Talk with the children about how fire trucks hook their hoses up to fire hydrants and spray water to put out fires.
3. Show the children the hoses, fire cutouts, and firefighter materials.
4. Invite the children to dress up as firefighters and work together to put out the fires they see.

TEACHER-TO-TEACHER TIP

- Take the children on a field trip to the local firehouse to see the fire trucks, firefighters (in regular clothing and firefighter gear), where firefighters live, what they do while at the firehouse, and to handle an actual fire hose.

ASSESSMENT

To assess the children's learning, consider the following:
- Do the children understand the importance of the fire department in the community?
- Are the children able to work together to put out the imaginary fires?

Children's Books

Curious George and the Firefighters by Margaret and H.A. Rey
A Day with Firefighters by Jan Kottke
Even Firefighters Hug Their Moms by Christine Kole MacLean

Tina Durham-Woehler, Lebanon, TN

Trash Pick Up and Recycling

3+

Materials

6 small wastebaskets (or plastic ice cream buckets)
6 "recycling bins" (plastic colored storage bins or shoeboxes)
1 larger garbage can
1 plastic milk crate
wagon
crumbled tissues
objects for recycling such as paper, aluminum, plastic, and so on

LEARNING OBJECTIVES

The children will:
1. Learn about trash collection and recycling collection.
2. Improve their self-confidence.
3. Develop their large motor skills.

VOCABULARY

collect	garbage	glass	paper
pick up	plastic	recycle	trash

PREPARATION

- Label the various bins "recycling" and "trash," and fill them with the appropriate materials.
- Display a bin and a basket together at six different locations in the classroom.
- Set the larger garbage can in the wagon along with a milk crate.

WHAT TO DO

1. Talk with the children about what garbage and recycling are, and where they come from. Explain how it is important to put each in its proper containers. Talk with the children about garbage and recycling collectors. Explain what they do.
2. Show the children the wagon and various garbage collection points set up in the classroom. Invite the children to work together to collect the garbage and recycling.
3. Challenge the children to sort the recyclable materials into various groups, such as paper, plastic, and aluminum. Encourage the children to discuss why certain things are garbage and others are recyclable.

ASSESSMENT

To assess the children's learning, consider the following:
- Do the children understand the importance of garbage and recycling collection?
- Can the children identify and separate garbage from recyclable materials?

Mary J. Murray, Mazomanie, WI

Children's Books

I Stink by Kate McMullan
Recycle Everyday! by Nancy Wallace
Smash! Mash! Crash! There Goes the Trash! by Barbara Odanaka
Too Much Garbage by Testa Fulvio

Crossing Guard

LEARNING OBJECTIVES

The children will:
1. Improve their social skills.
2. Develop self-confidence.
3. Improve their awareness of crossing guard duties.
4. Learn about safety.

Materials

red construction
  paper
tongue depressor
black or white
  marker
masking tape
fluorescent vest or
  crossing guard
  vest/jacket/belt

VOCABULARY

cars	crossing guard	crosswalk	lines
safety	stop sign	street	walk

PREPARATION

● Make a stop sign with the red paper, marker, and tongue depressor.
● Create a pretend crosswalk using the masking tape.

WHAT TO DO

1. Talk with the children about the crossing guard or other person in your neighborhood who keeps children safe while crossing the street.
2. Invite the children to share what they know about crossing the street safely.
3. Display the clothing a crossing guard might wear.
4. Allow different children to try on the vest or belt.
5. Demonstrate how to play the role of a crossing guard as you display the sign to stop traffic, then motion for the children to cross safely between the lines of the "crosswalk."
6. Allow small groups of children to work with the materials and role play the crossing guard who safely shuttles children from one side of the street to the other.

SONG

Crossing Guard by Mary J. Murray
(Tune: "Three Blind Mice")

Crossing guard,　　　　　　　　　*You help us to safely cross the street,*
Crossing guard,　　　　　　　　　*You help us to safely cross the street,*
We need you.　　　　　　　　　　*You help us to safely cross the street,*
We need you.　　　　　　　　　　*We thank you.*

Children's Books

Crossing Guard by
  Joann Macken
High Five Hank by Alan
  MacDonald
School Crossing Guards
  by Terri Diesels

ASSESSMENT

To assess the children's learning, consider the following:
● Do children work together and take turns?
● Do the children understand the importance of following a crossing guard's instructions?

Mary J. Murray, Mazomanie, WI

Drive a Fire Truck

4+

LEARNING OBJECTIVES

The children will:
1. Learn about the importance of fire departments.
2. Develop their motor skills.

Materials

large, empty box
2–4 small (6" x 12"
   x 4") cardboard
   boxes
scrap cardboard
   pieces
industrial scissors or
   utility knife (adult
   use only)
clear packing tape
2 pie tins (any size),
   for headlights
drop cloth or
   plastic tablecloths
tempera paint
paintbrushes
smocks
firefighter costumes
   and props

Children's Books

Big Frank's Fire Truck by
   Leslie McGuire
*Curious George and the
   Firefighters* by Margaret
   and H.A. Rey
*Eyewitness Readers:
   Firefighters* by DK
   Publishing
*If I Could Drive a Fire
   Truck* by Michael
   Teitelbaum

VOCABULARY

Dalmatian	emergency	firefighter	firehouse	hose
hydrant	ladder	pole	siren	water

PREPARATIONS

- Set the box down and cut out windows and doors, so the children can use it as a fire truck.
- Use cut scraps of cardboard to make ladder shapes, and attach them to the back of the truck.

WHAT TO DO

1. Talk with the children about fire trucks. Ask them about times they have seen fire trucks in the street. Ask the children what purpose fire trucks and fire departments serve in the community.
2. Show the children the large box and explain that they will be decorating it to look like a fire truck.
3. Set out smocks, paint, brushes, boxes, and other necessary materials, and invite the children to paint the box so it resembles a fire truck. Help when necessary.
4. After the fire truck is dry, invite the children to dress up as firefighters and explore their fire truck.

ASSESSMENT

To assess the children's learning, consider the following:
- Do the children understand the important service fire departments provide?
- Can the children work together to paint and decorate the fire truck?
- Can the children play together using the fire truck and fire department props?

Tina Durham-Woehler, Lebanon, TN

Home Improvement Store 4+

LEARNING OBJECTIVES

The children will:
1. Develop their vocabularies.
2. Learn about various tools and building materials.
3. Develop their math skills.

Materials

objects for building
and construction
pictures of objects
for building and
construction
2 aprons
2 name tags
shopping bags
cash register and
play money
sign that reads
*Building Supply
Store*
building and
construction
catalogs or store
newspaper flyers
price tags

VOCABULARY

build	buy	cash	machines	register
shop	store	supplies	tools	

PREPARATION

● Use the materials to set up a home improvement or building supply store in the dramatic play area. Display the sign and the selection of materials and supplies within the "store." Be sure to include some pieces of lumber or wood.

WHAT TO DO

1. Ask the children if they have ever seen people doing construction work on their homes or on their neighbors' homes. Talk about where the supplies for that work came from.
2. Show the children the Building Supply Store materials, and invite the children to explore them, role playing as employees or customers.
3. Encourage the children to have questions for the workers at the store, such as: "What would I need to build a garage," "How much wood do I need to build a fence for my dog," and "Can you show me where the tools are located?"
4. Challenge the children use the play money and cash register to pay and make change for the materials.

ASSESSMENT

To assess the children's learning, consider the following:
● Do the children show an understanding of why people go to building supply stores?
● Do the children interact well with one another?

> Mary J. Murray, Mazomanie, WI

Children's Books

Those Building Men by Angela Johnson
Tools by Holly Mann
Tools by Taro Miura
Tools by Ann Morris

Newspaper Delivery

4+

LEARNING OBJECTIVES

The children will:
1. Improve their large motor and small motor skills.
2. Develop their number-recognition skills.
3. Improve their interpersonal skills.

Materials

newspapers
rubber bands
plastic newspaper
   delivery bags
clean, dry half-
   gallon milk
   cartons
10 sheets of 12" x
   18" colored
   construction
   paper
markers
large cloth bag

VOCABULARY

address	box	bundle	door
fold	newspaper	rubber band	toss

PREPARATION

- Cut the top off each milk carton. Lay each carton on its side and tape it to a table to represent a newspaper delivery box. Add an address card to each rural newspaper box. Display these rural newspaper mail boxes randomly around the classroom.
- Attach the 10 sheets of colored paper to a wall, two feet apart, to represent front doors on homes. Print an address on each "door."

WHAT TO DO

1. Talk with the children about newspapers and the news, and how this service is important to the community.
2. Invite groups of children to fold sections of newspaper and insert each paper into a plastic bag or wrap it with a rubber band.
3. After folding the newspapers, suggest that the children role play delivering the paper to various houses in the city and in rural neighborhoods.
4. Invite a small group of children to carry the papers in the "newspaper bag," insert the papers into the rural mailboxes, and toss the papers on the steps in front of each "door" of the city homes.
5. Have children take turns delivering papers as they practice social skills and say good morning to various people in the neighborhood while they work.

Children's Books

The American Newsboy
  by Michael Burgan
Delivery by Anastasia
     Suen
The Furry News by
  Loreen Leedy

ASSESSMENT

To assess the children's learning, consider the following:
- Were the children able to fold and bag or band the newspapers?
- Do the children understand why people deliver and read newspapers?
- What kind of things did the children say to one another as they delivered the newspapers?

Mary J. Murray, Mazomanie, WI

Submarine Sandwich Shop

LEARNING OBJECTIVES

The children will:
1. Explore role-playing.
2. Improve their social skills.
3. Develop their basic math skills.

Materials

craft foam or construction paper in various colors
scissors (adult use only)
aprons
name tags
wax paper or manila paper
play money in $1 and $2 denominations
poster board and marker

VOCABULARY

bread	cheese	lettuce	meat
olives	sandwich	submarine	tomato

PREPARATION

- Cut play bread and various sandwich fixings from the colored craft foam or construction paper, such as tomato slices, onion slices, pickles, lettuce, slices of meat and cheese, black olives, and so on.
- Display signs that read "Neighborhood Sub Shop" and "Sub Sandwiches $1."
- If necessary, draw, photocopy, and cut out several copies of pretend $1 and $2 bills.

WHAT TO DO

1. Draw the children's attention to the dramatic play area. Talk with the children about times they have been to a submarine sandwich shop.
2. Show the children the materials, and invite the children to pretend they are working in a neighborhood sandwich shop.
3. Give examples of language the food service worker might use, such as: "How can I help you? What could I get for you today? What would you like on your sandwich?"
4. Using play $1 and $2 bills, challenge the children to pay and provide simple change.

SONG

I'm Working at the Sandwich Shop by Mary J. Murray
(Tune "I'm Picking Up a Baby Bumble Bee")
I'm working at the sandwich shop, come see
I'll make one for you and I'll make one for me.
I'm working at the sandwich shop, come see.
Mmmmmmm...they're good. (pretend to take a bite)

Children's Books

Carla's Sandwich by Debbie Herman
The Giant Jam Sandwich by John Vernon Lord
Sam's Sandwich by David Pelham
The Sandwich that Max Made by Marcia Vaghan

ASSESSMENT

To assess the children's learning, consider the following:
- Can the children name the various ingredients they are using to make their sandwiches?
- Can the children make change using pretend money?

Mary J. Murray, Mazomanie, WI

Who Lives in My Neighborhood?

4+

Materials

LEARNING OBJECTIVES

The children will:
1. Use their imaginations.
2. Imitate the jobs of various people who make up a neighborhood.

VOCABULARY

baker	banker	firefighter	grocer
librarian	neighborhood	police officer	

WHAT TO DO

1. Spend some time reading books about people who work in a neighborhood (see list to the left for suggestions).
2. With the children, discuss the different people necessary to make each neighborhood or community work.

3. Ask the children how they might go about imitating the work that these various professionals do. Provide the children with some examples, such as a baker rolling dough or baking bread in an imaginary oven.
4. Tell the children they will be taking turns acting out the duties of various professionals while the rest of the children guess the profession.
5. Select a child, whisper a profession to that child, and have the child imitate the work of that professional as the rest of the children say what profession it is.
6. When the children guess the profession, ask them what the child was doing that made them see what the profession was.
7. Repeat the process with another child.

ASSESSMENT

To assess the children's learning, consider the following:
- Can the children name several jobs of people in the neighborhood?
- Can the children describe the duties of the people in those jobs?
- Can the children explain why those jobs are necessary for the community to function?

Children's Books

Communities by Sarah L. Schuette
Franklin's Nighborhood by Paulette Bourgeois
My Neighborhood by Lisa Bullard
Neighborhood Helpers by Jennifer B. Gillis
Where Do I Live? by Neil Chesanow

Donna Alice Patton, Hillsboro, Ohio

Working in a Restaurant

LEARNING OBJECTIVES

The children will:

1. Learn about what purpose a restaurant serves in a community.
2. Develop their interpersonal skills.

Materials

pictures of people
working in
restaurants
chefs' hats and
aprons
plastic dishes and
bins or trays
menus
serving trays
toy food

VOCABULARY

busser	cashier	chef	customer	host
meal	serve	server	restaurant	

WHAT TO DO

1. Show the children the various pictures of people working in a restaurant. Ask the children if they have ever been in a restaurant and seen people doing similar things.
2. Ask the children to name the jobs the various people in the pictures have. Help the children if necessary.
3. Show the children the various materials, asking the children to identify each item.
4. Invite the children to choose various roles and explore the experience of working or visiting a restaurant.
5. Observe as the children experiment with these various roles. Discuss the various responsibilities of each role. Talk with the children about the importance of being polite and thoughtful with one another.

ASSESSMENT

To assess the children's learning, consider the following:

- Do the children understand the purpose of restaurants?
- Can the children identify various roles and responsibilities of people in a restaurant?
- Are the children able to work with one another in a friendly manner?

Children's Books

Meet My Neighbor, the Restaurant Owner by Joanna Harvey
Going to a Restaurant by Melinda Beth Radabaugh
Working at a Restaurant by Katie Marisco

Debbie Vilardi, Commack, NY

Fire! Fire!

3+

LEARNING OBJECTIVES

The children will:
1. Increase their language skills.
2. Improve memory skills.
3. Expand their verbal fluency.

Materials

VOCABULARY

community	fire truck	firefighter
neighborhood	safety	town crier

WHAT TO DO

1. Talk with the children about how towns and areas protect themselves from fire. Ask the children if they know who to call if there is a fire.
2. Explain to the children that there wasn't always an emergency number, or even a phone. Before phones, towns would rely on town criers to make information known. The town crier rang a bell to get attention, and then told the neighbors any important news. The fire engine was pulled by horses.

3. Teach the children this poem about the universal lure of fire engines, and how people have always wanted to see them.

Fire, Fire (Traditional)
"Fire! Fire!" yells the town crier;
"Where? Where?" says Mrs. Blair.
"It's downtown!" said Mrs. Brown.
"I'll go and see it!" said Mrs. Peewit.
"So will I!" said Mrs. Fry.

ASSESSMENT

To assess the children's learning, consider the following:
● Can the children tell you about the job of a town crier?
● How do people get information quickly today? (email, texting, telephone)

Anna Adeney, Hereford, United Kingdom

Children's Books

Big Frank's Fire Truck by Leslie McGuire
Fire! Fire! by Gail Gibbons
Firefighters by Norma Simon

Firefighters Are People

3+

LEARNING OBJECTIVES

The children will:
1. Learn about the service firefighters provide the community.
2. Learn not to be afraid of firefighters.
3. Develop their memory skills.

Materials

VOCABULARY

equipment	firefighters	helmet
safety	smoke	uniform

WHAT TO DO

1. Gather the children together and talk with them about firefighters. Ask the children if they have ever seen or heard a fire truck in the street. Ask the children what they think firefighters do.
2. Explain how firefighters help to keep the community safe, and that the children should not be afraid of firefighters, even when they are wearing their helmets and other protective equipment.
3. Teach the children the following song.

Firefighters Are People by Kristen Peters
(Tune: "Did You Ever See a Lassie?")
Have you ever seen firefighters,
Firefighters, firefighters?
Have you ever seen firefighters,
Out of uniform?
They are fathers.
They are mothers.
They are brothers.
They are sisters.
Did you ever see a firefighter,
Out of uniform?

ASSESSMENT

To assess the children's learning, consider the following:
- Can the children describe how firefighters help the community?
- Can the children sing the song above?
- Do the children know not to be afraid of firefighters?

Kristen Peters, Mattituck, NY

Children's Books

A Day With Firefighters by Jan Kottke
Even Firefighters Hug Their Moms by Christine Kole Maclean
I'm a Firefighter by Mary Packard

Here in the Neighborhood 3+

LEARNING OBJECTIVES

The children will:
1. Learn a new song.
2. Discuss the importance of quiet when trying to rest.
3. Develop their observation skills.

Materials

VOCABULARY

community   friends   neighbors
neighborhood   quiet   rest

WHAT TO DO

1. Talk with the children about nighttime, and how at night most people in a community settle down for a good long rest.

2. Talk with the children about their nightly routines, and ask them if they need it to be quiet to fall asleep. Would they be able to sleep if their neighbor were playing a trumpet outside their bedroom window?

3. Teach the children the following song, emphasizing the importance of quiet:

   Here in the Neighborhood by Susan Oldham Hill
   (Tune: "You Are My Sunshine")
   Here in the neighborhood, it's time to rest, now.
   It's time to put our work away.
   We're getting quiet, neighbors are resting;
   If you listen, you can hear our neighbors say....
   (Repeat song)

4. Repeat the song with the children several times, singing it more quietly with each repetition. Consider making mats available and having the children lie down by the end of the song.

Children's Books

Clifford and the Grouchy Neighbors by Norman Bridwell
Everybody Cooks Rice by Norah Dooley
Louie's Search by Ezra Jack Keats

ASSESSMENT

To assess the children's learning, consider the following:
- Do the children appreciate the importance of a neighborhood being quiet at night?
- Can the children repeat the song more quietly, as prompted?

Susan Oldham Hill, Lakeland, FL

Hi, Neighbor

3+

LEARNING OBJECTIVES

The children will:
1. Learn the value of greeting others.
2. Practice different ways to greet others.

Materials

VOCABULARY

community   friends   greet
neighbor   neighborhood   polite

WHAT TO DO

1. Explain to the children that a neighbor is anyone who lives near where they live. A neighbor could be someone who lives or works in their town. Ask for examples of neighbors, such as store workers, police, letter carriers, people next door, and so on.

2. Discuss different ways to say hello, or greet people, in a friendly way (smile, wave, shake hands, speak with kindness), and why it is important to be friendly to neighbors.

3. Teach the following song with all the motions:

Hi, Neighbor by Kay Flowers
(Tune: "Head and Shoulders, Knees and Toes, Knees and Toes")
I smile at people that I see...on the street. (trace smile on face with fingers)
I wave to neighbors that I meet...on the street, (wave to one another)
Being friendly is the proper way to greet; (shake hands with those on either side)
So smile at people on your street...on your street. (smile and wave)

TEACHER-TO-TEACHER TIP

- Use this song as a fun transition as children walk from one activity to another, down a hallway, or out to the playground.

ASSESSMENT

To assess the children's learning, consider the following:
- Do the children greet others outside their own classroom?
- Can the children sing the song and do the appropriate motions?

Kay Flowers, Summerfield, OH

Children's Books

Do Something in Your City by Amanda Rondeau
My Neighborhood by Lisa Bullard
Night on Neighborhood Street by Eloise Greenfield
Only One Neighborhood by Marc Harshman
Where Do I Live? by Neil Chesanow

In My Community

3+

LEARNING OBJECTIVES

The children will:

1. Name familiar places in their community.
2. Sing a simple song with the aid of flannel board song props.

Materials

flannel board
pictures of places
    mentioned in the
    song

VOCABULARY

community	gas station	grocery store	library
mall	pet store	restaurant	video store

WHAT TO DO

1. Talk with the children about various places in their community that they go on a regular basis.
2. Teach the children the following song. Show the children a picture of the location prior to singing the verse about that location. (Invite the children to think of new places and bring in pictures to add to the song.)

In My Community by Jackie Wright
(Tune "Here We Go 'Round the Mulberry Bush")

*I can go to the grocery
    store,
The grocery store, the
    grocery store.
I can go to the grocery
    store
In my community.*

*I can go to the pet store,
The pet store, the pet
    store.
I can go to the pet store
In my community.*

*I can go to the gas station,
The gas station, the gas
    station.
I can go to the gas station
In my community.*

*I can go to the library,
The library, the library.
I can go to the library
In my community.*

*I can go to a restaurant,
A restaurant, a restaurant.
I can go to a restaurant
In my community.*

*I can go to the mall,
To the mall, to the mall.
I can go to the mall
In my community.*

ASSESSMENT

To assess the children's learning, consider the following:

● Can the children identify various places in their community in pictures?
● Are the children able to remember the song from verse to verse?

Jackie Wright, Enid, OK

Children's Books

*Do Something in Your
    City* by Amanda
    Rondeau
My Neighborhood by
    Lisa Bullard
*Only One
Neighborhood* by Marc
    Harshman
Where Do I Live? by
    Neil Chesanow
Whose Hat Is This? by
    Katz Cooper

I've Been Picking Up the Garbage

3+

Materials

LEARNING OBJECTIVES

The children will:
1. Learn about an important community service.
2. Develop their memory skills.

VOCABILARY

clean-up   compactor   garbage   pick up   recycle   trash

WHAT TO DO

1. Talk with the children about garbage. Ask them what garbage is and where it goes. Have the children seen garbage collectors in their neighborhoods?
2. Sing the following song with the children:

   I Am Picking Up the Garbage by Mary J. Murray
   (Tune: "I've Been Working on the Railroad")
   I am picking up the garbage, all along the way.
   I am picking up recyclables, it's how I spend my day.
   Helping people in the neighborhood.
   I rise up early in the morning.
   Helping people in the neighborhood. I'm glad I get to help.

TRS Company
Trash Removal
Service

ASSESSMENT

To assess the children's learning, consider the following:
- Do the children understand what trash collectors do?
- Can the children sing the song?

Mary J. Murray, Mazomanie, WI

Children's Books

I Stink by Kate McMullan
Recycle Everyday! by Nancy Wallace
Smash! Mash! Crash! There Goes the Trash! by Barbara Odanaka
Too Much Garbage by Testa Fulvio

Let's Build a House

3+

LEARNING OBJECTIVES

The children will:
1. Develop their memory and recall capabilities.
2. Learn about how houses and apartments are built.

Materials

sample objects
people in the
song would use

VOCABULARY

architect   chimney   landscaper   painter
pound   sweeper   welder

WHAT TO DO

1. Gather the children together and lead them in a discussion about their homes, asking them how houses and apartment buildings get built.
2. Teach the children the following poem. Consider teaching only one or two verses each day, and adding them together over the course of a week, so that the children can recite the entire poem at the week's end.

Let's Build a House by Jackie Wright

Let's build a house.
Let's build a house.
Let's build a house,
And work, work, work.

I'll be the architect.
I'll be the architect.
I'll be the architect.
And draw, draw, draw.

I'll build some walls.
I'll build some walls.
I'll build some walls,
And pound, pound,
*   pound.*

I'll be the painter.
I'll be the painter.
I'll be the painter,
And paint, paint,
*   paint.*

I'll be the plumber.
I'll be the plumber.
I'll be the plumber,
And work, work, work.

I'll be the sweeper.
I'll be the sweeper.
I'll be the sweeper,
And sweep, sweep,
*   sweep.*

I'll build the chimney.
I'll build the chimney.
I'll build the chimney,
And work, work, work.

I'll be the welder.
I'll be the welder.
I'll be the welder,
And weld, weld, weld.

I'll be the landscaper.
I'll be the landscaper.
I'll be the landscaper,
And plant, plant,
*   plant.*

ASSESSMENT

To assess the children's learning, consider the following:
- Do the children understand how homes and buildings are made?
- Can the children remember the verses of the poem from one day to the next?

Jackie Wright, Enid, OK

Children's Books

Alphabet Under Construction by Denise Fleming
Building a House by Byron Barton
The Toolbox by Anne Rockwell

Let's Go, Neighbor

3+

LEARNING OBJECTIVES

The children will:
1. Learn to be polite when talking with their neighbors.
2. Develop their memory skills.

Materials

VOCABULARY

friendly   neighbor   polite   transition

WHAT TO DO

1. When it is time to begin a transition in the classroom, ask one child to tap five "neighbors" gently on the shoulder and say, "Let's go, neighbor," as an indicator to line up.
2. Encourage each child tapped by the first child to find another neighbor, hold hands, and prepare to transition to the next activity.
3. Teach children the following song. Use this song when children need to clean up at the end of one activity.

Can You Find a Neighbor by Susan Oldham Hill
(Tune: "Do You Know the Muffin Man?")
Oh, can you find a neighbor who
Will put our things away with you?
Oh, can you find a neighbor who
Will help put things away?

Oh, can you find a neighbor who
Likes neighborhoods to look
  brand new?
Oh, find a neighbor who will help
Put everything away.

ASSESSMENT

To assess the children's learning, consider the following:
- Are the children friendly when talking with their "neighbors"?
- Do the children transition on to the next activity effectively?

Susan Oldham Hill, Lakeland, FL

Children's Books

The Big Orange Splot by D. Manus Pinkwater
Clifford and the Grouchy Neighbors by Norman Bridwell
Everybody Cooks Rice by Norah Dooley
Louie's Search by Ezra Jack Keats

People Day and Night

3+

LEARNING OBJECTIVES

The children will:
1. Learn that not every job ends at night.
2. Learn some of the people who work each night.
3. Develop their listening skills.

Materials

VOCABULARY

emergency   maintenance   nocturnal   shift   worker

WHAT TO DO

1. Read the children one or more of the books about people who work at night (for book suggestions, see the list to the left).
2. Talk with the children about people who work at night. Ask the children if they have ever been out at night and seen people working. Ask them what kinds of jobs those people were doing.
3. Discuss the types of jobs that go on all night long and how the people who work these jobs make our neighborhoods better places.
4. Recite the following poem with the children:

Who Works at Night? by Anonymous
While I'm in bed asleep
At night and dreaming of sheep

People are working to keep
Our streets safe and clean.

Garbage collectors pick up the trash.
Nurses help to heal your rash.

Police officers walk the streets.
Taxi drivers bring folks home to sleep.

So many people work all night
Until the night's first light.

Children's Books

Frankie Works the Night Shift by Lisa Westberg Peters
A Good Night Walk by Elisha Cooper
Night Shift by Jessie Hartland
The Night Worker by Kate Banks

ASSESSMENT

To assess the children's learning, consider the following:
- Can the children identify jobs that people do at night?
- Can the children say why it is important for the community to have people who work at night?

Sue Bradford Edwards, Florissant, MO

Serving Lunch

3+

LEARNING OBJECTIVES

The children will:
1. Learn about eating in restaurants.
2. Develop their memory skills.

Materials

VOCABULARY

| food | lunch | menu | restaurant |
| quesadilla | serve | spaghetti | |

WHAT TO DO

1. Talk with the children about experiences they have had eating lunch in restaurants. Ask the children what kinds of foods they like to eat in restaurants.
2. Ask the children about the people they saw working in the restaurants they have visited. Can they name the different jobs of the people they saw there?
3. Recite the following poem with the children:

Serving Lunch by Laura Wynkoop
Let's serve up lots of yummy food,
Spaghetti, mac 'n' cheese,
Corn dogs, pizza, chicken strips
With corn and buttered peas,
Chili fries and quesadillas,
Burgers by the bunch,
Just tell us what you'd like to have,
And we will serve you lunch!

ASSESSMENT

To assess the children's learning, consider the following:
- Can the children recite the poem?
- Can the children recall specific foods they have eaten for lunch in restaurants?

Laura Wynkoop, San Dimas, CA

Children's Books

Froggy Eats Out by Jonathan London
Going to a Restaurant by Melinda Beth Radabaugh
Restaurant Owners by Cecilia Minden and Mary Minden Zins

This Is the Way They Build My House

3+

Materials

LEARNING OBJECTIVES

The children will:

1. Learn about the people who build homes.
2. Develop their vocabulary.

VOCABULARY

bricklayer	builder	carpenter	digger	electrician
glazier	painter	plasterer	plumber	roofer

WHAT TO DO

1. Ask the children to describe the homes or apartments in which they live.
2. Explain that all buildings are made by various people who have different jobs. These people work together to give everyone a place to live.
3. Name various construction jobs people have, and explain what those workers do. Have the children repeat the names of the jobs.
4. Sing the following song with the children:

This Is the Way They Build My House by Anne Adeney
(Tune: "Here We Go Gathering Nuts in May")
(chorus)
This is the way they build my house,
Build my house, build my house.
This is the way they build my house;
A fine new house for me.

(verse)
First the digger digs a big hole, digs a big
*   hole, digs a big hole.*
First the digger digs a big hole, for a fine
*   new house for me.*

(additional verses)
The mixer churns the gray concrete...

The builder pours concrete into the hole...
The bricklayer lays bricks to build the
*   walls...*
The carpenter cuts wood to line the
*   walls...*
The electrician puts the wiring in...
The plumber puts in all the pipes...
The glazier puts all the windows in...
The plasterer smoothes off all the walls...
The painter paints in bright, cool colors...
The roofer puts tiles on the roof...
This is the way they build my house...

ASSESSMENT

To assess the children's learning, consider the following:

- Can the children recognize the job when you tell them the name of the worker?
- Can the children name many of the workers necessary to build a house?

Anna Adeney, Hereford, United Kingdom

Children's Books

Construction Site by
Lola M. Schafer
Men at Work by Lewis
Wickes Hine
Building a House by
Byron Barton

Trucks, Trucks Everywhere 3+

LEARNING OBJECTIVES
The children will:
1. Learn about trucks that help provide services in the neighborhood.
2. Participate as a group in the chant.
3. Describe the function of trucks mentioned in the chant.

Materials
pictures or models
  of trucks
markers, crayons,
  and colored
  pencils
glitter
glue
stickers
other art materials

VOCABULARY
delivery   logo   service   transportation

PREPARATION
● Make several simple construction paper cutouts of various types of trucks. Use cut out photos as outline models.

WHAT TO DO
1. Gather the children together and engage them in a discussion about various kinds of trucks they are familiar with.
2. Show the children the pictures of the trucks and challenge the children to name the different types of trucks.
3. Teach the children the following poem:

So Many Trucks by Margery Kranyik Fermino
Pick-up trucks, fire trucks, dump trucks, go,
How many other trucks do we know?
Trash trucks, trailer trucks, old and new,
Small trucks, large trucks, red, white and blue.

Pick-up trucks, fire trucks, dump trucks, tow trucks,
Oil trucks, mail trucks, ice cream trucks, WOW!
All around the neighborhood, up hill and down,
Trucks are helping us all around the town.

4. Show the children the construction paper truck cutouts and other various art materials. Invite the children to begin constructing and decorating their own trucks.
5. Talk with the children about their trucks as they decorate them. Ask the children what kind of trucks they are working on.

ASSESSMENT
To assess the children's learning, consider the following:
● Can the children name different types of trucks?
● Are the children able to decorate their cutouts of different trucks in recognizable ways?

Margery Kranyik Fermino, West Roxbury, MA

Children's Books
I Love Trucks by
Philemon Sturges,
My Big Truck Book by
Roger Priddy
Trucks Board Book by
Byron Burton

Five Nice Neighbors

4+

LEARNING OBJECTIVES

The children will:
1. Learn to recognize numerals.
2. Develop their understanding of basic number order.

Materials

chart with the
  words to the
  fingerplay
large numeral cards
  from 1–5

VOCABULARY

chime	community	doorbell
home	neighbor	neighborhood

WHAT TO DO

1. Talk with the children about the people they know in their neighborhood. Explain to the children that the people who live nearby are called "neighbors."
2. Teach the children the following fingerplay:

Five Nice Neighbors by Susan Oldham Hill
Five nice neighbors in the neighborhood. (hold up all five fingers on one hand)
Acting kind and friendly like neighbors should.
The first nice neighbor helped someone build a wall. (point one finger in the air)
The second neighbor helped a girl find her big, red ball. (point two fingers in the air)
The third nice neighbor helped a lady wash her car. (point three fingers in the air)
And the fourth nice neighbor taught the boys to play guitar. (point four fingers in the air)
The fifth nice neighbor fixed someone's doorbell chime, (point five fingers in the air)
And they all went out to dinner and had a great time!

3. After reciting the fingerplay with the children, show them the large numeral cards. Explain that each card indicates a specific number.
4. Select five children, and have them stand in front of the class, holding the cards in order from one to five.
5. Recite the fingerplay with the children again, having each child hold up the appropriate card when the children say that number.

ASSESSMENT

To assess the children's learning, consider the following:
- Can the children recite the fingerplay?
- Can the children hold up the correct number of fingers at the appropriate time?
- Can the children holding the number cards wave them at the appropriate time?

Susan Oldham Hill, Lakeland, FL

Children's Books

The Big Orange Splot by D. Manus Pinkwater
Clifford and the Grouchy Neighbors by Norman Bridwell
Everybody Cooks Rice by Norah Dooley
Louie's Search by Ezra Jack Keats

Icy Cold Alaska

4+

LEARNING OBJECTIVES

The children will:

1. Learn about Alaska.
2. Identify Alaska on a North American map.
3. Memorize a poem.

Materials

North American
map

VOCABULARY

| Alaska | cold | ice | polar bear | snow | state |

WHAT TO DO

1. Show the children a map of North America. Point out where the continental United States is. Show the children that the United States also includes Hawai'i and Alaska.
2. Ask the children what they think life is like in Alaska. Is it warm? Is it cold? Do the children know what kinds of animals might live there?
3. Recite the following poem with the children:

Alaska by Shirley Anne Ramaley
*Part of Alaska is icy cold
That is what I am told.*

*An arctic fox and a polar bear,
I know they both live there.*

*Lots of snow and lots of ice.
I think that is pretty nice.*

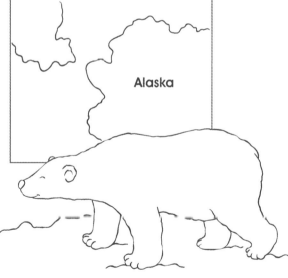

Alaska

ASSESSMENT

To assess the children's learning, consider the following:

* Can the children identify Alaska on a North American map?
* Were the children able to memorize and recite the poem?

Shirley Anne Ramaley, Sun City, AZ

Children's Books

Alaska by Shelley Gill and Patrick J. Endres
Alaska ABC Book by Charlene Kreeger and Shannon Cartwright
Alaska's Three Pigs by Arlene Laverde and Mindy Dwyer
Count Alaska's Colors by Shelley Gill and Shannon Cartwright

Neighborhood Match

4+

LEARNING OBJECTIVES

The children will:
1. Learn about the importance of helping neighbors.
2. Identify various tools.
3. Develop their memory skills.

Materials

pictures of or actual tools, such as hammers, rakes, shovels, and so on

VOCABULARY

favor	hammer	help	lend
neighbor	rake	shovel	

WHAT TO DO

1. Talk with the children about their neighbors. Ask the children if they have ever seen family members help or receive help from a neighbor on a project, like raking the yard, shoveling snow, or some construction project.
2. Tell the children that this kind of neighborly friendliness is an important part of what makes a community work.
3. Teach the children following song:

Neighbor, Neighbor by Susan Oldham Hill
(Tune: "Daisy, Daisy")
Neighbor, neighbor,
Give me your answer, do.
What's the tool I use when I'm helping you?
I come to your house to help you;
My special tools come with me.
So here's a game: Now, can you name
The special tool that I use.

4. Show the children the pictures or samples of the different tools and ask them to identify each and talk about how people would use the tools to help their neighbors.

ASSESSMENT

To assess the children's learning, consider the following:
- Do the children understand the importance of being good neighbors?
- Can the children identify the various tools?
- Are the children able to recite the song?

Children's Books

Delivering Your Mail: A Book About Mail Carriers by Ann Owen
Franklin's Neighborhood by Paulette Bourgeois
Jobs Around My Neighborhood by Gladys Rosa-Mendoza
Katy and the Big Snow by Virginia Lee Burton

Susan Oldham Hill, Lakeland, FL

Neighbors Helping

4+

LEARNING OBJECTIVES

The children will:
1. Learn about the importance of helping their neighbors.
2. Develop their memory skills.

Materials

VOCABULARY

favor   friendly   help   neighbor   neighborhood

WHAT TO DO

With the children, sing the following song. Choose one child to be the neighbor helping in each verse, and invite that child to make up motions that indicate the helping action. At the end, have all the neighbors hold hands and sing together.

The Neighbor Next Door by Susan Oldham Hill
(Tune: "Do You Know the Muffin Man?")

Oh, have you seen the man next door?
Mr. Fitch, the man next door.
Oh, have you seen the man next door?
He helps me mow the lawn.

There's a girl across the street.
Susannah lives across the street.
Oh, there's a girl across the street:
She helps me walk my dog.

A lady lives in the big, brown house.
Mrs. Alexander in the big, brown house.
She lives in her big, brown house,
She always says, "Hello."

A boy lives across our backyard fence.
Antwon lives across our fence

He lives across our backyard fence;
He taught me how to skate.

A nice man lives just two doors down.
Mr. Lopez lives just two doors down
A nice man lives just two doors down
He helped Dad change our tire.

A lady lives way down the road.
Mrs. Yokohama lives way down the road.
A lady lives way down the road;
She brings us apple pie.

The people in my neighborhood.
My neighborhood, my neighborhood,
The people in my neighborhood
Are all good friends of mine!

ASSESSMENT

To assess the children's learning, consider the following:
- Are the children able to sing the song?
- Can the children identify the favors the neighbors perform in the song?

Susan Oldham Hill, Lakeland, FL

Children's Books

Everybody Brings Noodles by Norah Dooley
Louie's Search by Ezra Jack Keats
Qunito's Neighborhood by Ina Cumpiano
Who Are the People in Your Neighborhood? by Naomi Kleinberg

This Home Is My Home

4+

LEARNING OBJECTIVES

The children will:
1. Discuss the importance of sharing space at home and in the classroom.
2. Learn and sing a song.

Materials

VOCABULARY

home   house   play   share   sleep   work

WHAT TO DO

1. Talk with the children about their homes. Ask the children who they live with, and if they share rooms or bathrooms with siblings.
2. Talk about how important it is to know how to share space. Point out to the children that they share space together in the classroom. Explain that sharing space happens everywhere in the community.
3. Teach the children the following song:

   This Home Is My Home by Susan Oldham Hill
   (Tune: "This Land Is Your Land")
   This home is your home,
   This home is my home;
   We work and play here,
   We sleep and stay here;
   It is not mystery
   That we're a family;
   This home was made for you and me.

ASSESSMENT

To assess the children's learning, consider the following:
● Do the children understand the importance of sharing space with others?
● Can the children sing the song?

Susan Oldham Hill, Lakeland, FL

Children's Books

A Chair for My Mother by Vera Williams
City by Numbers by Stephen Johnson
City Lullaby by Marilyn Singer

Where Do They Belong?

4+

LEARNING OBJECTIVES

The children will:

1. Learn the names of various professions.
2. Identify the locations where people do their work.
3. Understand that pictures and symbols have meaning, and that print carries a message.

Materials

pictures of different people working
pictures of the places where these people work

VOCABULARY

astronaut	doctor	garbage collector	garbage truck
hospital	police officer	police station	post office
postal worker	president	space ship	taxi cab
taxi driver	white house		

PREPARATION

- Make red and green signs to resemble stoplights.
- Make a list of the people.
- Make copies of the song.

WHAT TO DO

1. Gather the children together. Show the children the various pictures of people and the places where they work.
2. Help the children identify the various people and where they work.
3. Explain that it is important for all of these people to do their jobs in order for the world to function smoothly.
4. Ask the children which profession they want to have when they grow up.
5. Sing the following song with the children:

   Where Do They Go? by Carol Hupp
   (Tune: "Mary Had a Little Lamb")
   Where does the _____ go, (name a person or object)
   The _____ go, the _____ go?
   Where does the _____ go?
   He/She goes in the _____.

ASSESSMENT

To assess the children's learning, consider the following:

- Can the children name the various professions of the people in the pictures?
- Can the children match the professions to the correct places of work?
- Do the children understand what each profession does to help society?

Children's Books

Jobs Around My Neighborhood by Gladys Rosa-Mendoza
Jobs on a Farm by Nancy Dickmann
Jobs People Do by Felicity Brooks

Carol Hupp, Farmersville, IL

Where Would You Rather Live?

4+

Materials

pictures of various types of communities

LEARNING OBJECTIVES

The children will:

1. Learn about different kinds of communities.
2. Develop social awareness.
3. Sing a simple song.

VOCABULARY

apartment	city	farm
house	mobile home	rural community
small town	suburban community	urban neighborhood

WHAT TO DO

1. Engage the children in a discussion about where different people live. Show the children the pictures of different locations.
2. Ask the children if they have lived in or visited different kinds of places in their lives, and talk about those places.
3. Discuss how cities, suburbs, small towns, and rural areas are different from each other.
4. Ask the children to think about those four choices and to say where they would like to live. Ask them to describe why they would choose one place over the other.
5. Sing the following song with the children. Each time the class sings the song, choose one of the children to say where he wants to live.

Where You Want to Live by Jackie Wright
(Tune: "Here We Go 'Round the Mulberry Bush")

Please, tell us where you want to live   (child's name), *tell us where you*
Want to live, want to live.   *want to live*
Please, tell us where you want to   *Want to live, want to live.*
    live.   (child's name), *tell us where you*
We would really like to know.   *want to live.*
                                                                        We would really like to know.

Children's Books

My Town by Rebecca Treays
Town Mouse, Country Mouse by Jan Brett
Where Do I Live? by Neil Chesanow

ASSESSMENT

To assess the children's learning, consider the following:

- Do the children understand that there are different types of communities?
- Can the children describe the characteristics of different types of communities?
- Which types of communities do the children want to live in? Why?

Jackie Wright, Enid, OK

USA Puzzles

4+

LEARNING OBJECTIVES

The children will:
1. Complete puzzles of the United States of America.
2. Develop their visual discrimination skills.

laminated maps of
    the United States
    of America
scissors (adult use
    only)
zip-lock bags

RELATED VOCABULARY

country	jigsaw	map
puzzle	state	United States of America

PREPARATION

● Cut each laminated map into pieces to make a simple jigsaw puzzle. Cut along state lines to create several pieces, depending on the age and ability of the children. Place each set of puzzle pieces in a zip-lock bag.

WHAT TO DO

1. Display a large classroom map of the United States of America. Point out that our country is made up of 50 different states. See if the children can identify the state they live in. Ask the children if they have visited other states. Identify states on the map that children have visited.
2. Tell the children that they will be putting together jigsaw puzzles of the United States of America. Give each child a set of puzzle pieces and have them complete the puzzles.

TEACHER-TO-TEACHER TIP

● When cutting the maps into puzzle pieces, make each set a little different. Vary the size and shape of the pieces, as well as the number of pieces in each puzzle. Once the children have completed their puzzles, they can trade with others.

ASSESSMENT

To assess the children's learning, consider the following:
● Can the children identify the state they live in?
● Can the children complete their puzzles with minimal or no help?

Laura Wynkoop, San Dimas, CA

Children's Books

A to Z United States of America by Jeff Reynolds
Postcards from the United States by Denise Allard
The United States ABCs: A Book About the People and Places of the United States of America by Holly Schroeder and Jeff Yesh

What Job Do I Do?

4+

LEARNING OBJECTIVES

The children will:
1. Identify some occupations they might see in their neighborhood.
2. Relate professions to the tools of those professions.
3. Engage in dramatic play.

Materials

envelopes
baker's apron,
   bowl, and
   wooden spoon
order pad and pen
police badge and
   hat
toy doctor's kit

VOCABULARY

baker   firefighter   occupation   police officer   waitress/waiter

WHAT TO DO

1. Engage the children in a discussion about various professions. Talk about what police officers, doctors, waiters in restaurants, and bakers do. Explain how each one of these professions is important to the community.
2. Choose four children and tell them they will be playing a police officer, a doctor, a waiter, or a baker. Whisper one of the professions to each child.
3. Set out the various items related to each profession, but do not have the children playing the roles pick them up or put them on.
4. Have the children act out their given roles in some way in front of the rest of the class.
5. After each child finishes acting out a profession, the rest of the children choose which items the child acting out that profession would use, and then name the profession.
6. Continue playing with four new children.

TEACHER-TO-TEACHER TIP

- To extend this activity, ask the children to think of other jobs people in their neighborhoods do, including dance teacher, florist, book seller, and so on. Invite the children to look for items that might indicate these professions, and then act out the jobs, challenging the remaining children to guess the profession.

ASSESSMENT

To assess the children's learning, consider the following:
- Can the children act out aspects of the various professions?
- Can the children associate the correct items with their professions?

Children's Books

Delivering Your Mail by
   Ann Owen
On the Town by
   Judith Caseley
Sidewalk Trip by
   Patricia Hubbell

Sue Bradford Edwards, Florissant, MO

Occupations Memory Cards

5

Materials

pictures of people in various professions
card stock paper
scissors (adult use only)
pencil
crayons
colored pencils or markers

LEARNING OBJECTIVES

The children will:
1. Learn to identify various occupations.
2. Develop their memory skills.

VOCABULARY

astronaut	bus driver	chef	doctor	firefighter
mail carrier	nurse	police officer	teacher	

PREPARATION

- Cut out the pictures of people in various professions.
- Make color photocopies of each so there are pairs of all the pictures.
- Paste each individual picture to identical pieces of card stock paper.

WHAT TO DO

1. Gather a few children together and lead them in a discussion about various people who have important jobs in the community.
2. Ask the children to say what kinds of jobs they want to have when they grow up. Talk with the children about why certain jobs are necessary and what they contribute to the community.
3. Show the children the occupation cards.
4. Set out the pairs of cards face-down in two rows in front of the children.
5. Have one child pick a first card, flip it over, and say what profession the picture shows.
6. Have a second child flip a second card and identify its profession. Ask the children if the professions match. If they do, leave the two cards face up. If they do not match, put the two cards face down.
7. Have the children continue to do this until they have found and identified all the matching pairs.

ASSESSMENT

To assess the children's learning, consider the following:
- Can the children identify the various occupations listed on the cards?
- Are the children able to remember the locations of and match the various occupation cards?

Children's Books

Career Day by Anne Rockwell
Jobs Around My Neighborhood by Gladys Rosa-Mendoza
When I Grow Up by P.K. Hallinan

Mayra Calvani, Belgium

Delivering ABC's Mail

4+

LEARNING OBJECTIVES

The children will:
1. Learn the first letters in the names of various objects.
2. Familiarize themselves with the postal service.

Materials

mail carrier bags
images of objects,
   animals, and so
   on
glue stick
26 index cards
26 cardboard
   "mail" boxes,
   each with a letter
   from A to Z
   written on it

VOCABULARY

alphabet   delivery   mail carrier   post office

PREPARATION

- On each index card, paste a colored picture of an object. Be sure that each object's name starts with a different letter of the alphabet. Write the first letter of each object's name on the back of its card.

WHAT TO DO

1. Ask the children if they have ever received a letter or package in the mail. Ask the children how the mail carrier knew to deliver their mail or packages to them.
2. Show the children the alphabet mail and mailboxes. Explain that each picture is addressed to a specific mailbox. Point out the letters on the mailboxes, as well as the letters on the backs of the cards. With the children, identify the objects on the fronts of the cards, and explain that the letters on the backs of the cards are the first letters in the objects' names.
3. Give each child a few cards in a "mail" bag and invite the children to take turns being mail carriers who deliver the letters to the correct mailboxes.

SONG

The Mail Carrier by Kristen Peters   (Tune "Are You Sleeping?")

There's the mail carrier.   *Is it a postcard,*
There's the mail carrier.   *Or a box or letter.*

Mail for me?   *What can it be?*
Mail for me?   *What can it be?*

Children's Books

A to Z by Sandra
   Boynton
ABC I Like Me! by
   Nancy Carlson
Delivering Your Mail by
   Ann Owen
*The Post Office Book:
Mail and How It Moves*
   by Gail Gibbons

ASSESSMENT

To assess the children's learning, consider the following:
- Do the children have a basic understanding of how the postal system works?
- Can the children put the mail in the correct mailboxes?

Kristen Peters, Mattituck, NY

Flag Riddles

4+

LEARNING OBJECTIVES

The children will:
1. Learn the colors of the flag.
2. Develop their large motor skills.

Materials

American flag
white construction
  paper
markers and
  crayons
glue
pre-cut white stars

VOCABULARY

America   blue   flag   red   symbol   white

WHAT TO DO

1. Display the American flag for the children and lead them in a discussion about its colors and shapes. Explain that the flag is a symbol of our country.

2. Ask the children what part of the flag these riddles describe:

   My color is white and I rest on the blue.
   I have five points and I shine brightly, too. (star)

   I am a rectangle on the far left side.
   My color is blue and I'm built with pride. (blue field)

   I am a stripe the color of snow.
   I go from side to side on our flag, you know. (white stripe)

   Courage is my color and I'm bright and strong.
   I run across the flag: I'm short AND long. (red stripe)

3. Set out the paper, crayons, and glue and invite the children to try making copies of the American flag, or simply try making up new kinds of flags using these materials.

ASSESSMENT

To assess the children's learning, consider the following:
- Can the children identify the American flag as a national symbol?
- Can the children name the colors on the flag, as well as its other components (stripes and stars)?

Susan Oldham Hill, Lakeland, FL

Children's Books

America the Beautiful by Katharine Lee Bates and Neil Waldman
F Is for Flag by Wendy Cheyette Lewison
How Many Days to America?: A Thanksgiving Story by Eve Bunting

My Community from A to Z

4+

Materials

digital camera
computer and
    printer
notebook
pencil or pen
scissors (adult use
    only)
glue
paper

LEARNING OBJECTIVES

The children will:
1. Learn about their community.
2. Develop their understanding of the alphabet.

VOCABULARY

alphabet	billboard	bus
community	field trip	landmark

PREPARATION

- Send home permission forms for a field trip through the local community. Explain that the children will get off the bus to take pictures.
- Consult the local phone book to help locate signs that contain all the letters of the alphabet.

WHAT TO DO

1. Talk with the children about the alphabet and how it is comprised of 26 different letters. Recite the alphabet with the children.
2. Tell the children they will be going on an alphabet trip.
3. Go on a walk or bus ride through the local area, pointing out the various letters on signs, from A–Z, and taking pictures of them. Note the context in which the letter is located. Is it a store sign? A billboard? A landmark? Have different children stand in each picture.
4. After getting pictures of all the letters, return to the classroom and print the pictures in a size no smaller than 4" x 6". Paste the pictures on construction paper, writing the letter the children found on each page.
5. Make a book from the pictures, modeled after *City Seen from A to Z* by Rachel Isadora.
6. Add the book to the classroom library, inviting the children to look through it and describe the letters and the experience of finding them.

ASSESSMENT

To assess the children's learning, consider the following:
- Can the children recite the letters of the alphabet?
- Were the children able to see the letters on the signs in the community?

Children's Books

City Seen From A to Z
    by Rachel Isadora
Communities by Gail
    Saunders-Smith
Everyone Makes a
Difference by Cindy
    Leaney
My Neighborhood by
    Lisa Bullard

Virginia Jean Herrod, Columbia, SC

Neighborhood Alphabet

4+

LEARNING OBJECTIVES

The children will:
1. Begin recognizing letters of the alphabet.
2. Practice saying letters of the alphabet.

Materials

alphabet cards
pictures
chart

VOCABULARY

address   block   entrance   recycle   sign   U-turn

PREPARATION

● Make a chart with these words and their matching initial letters:

a address	j July 4th party	s sandbox
b block	k kids	t trees
c corner	l library	u U-turn
d driveway	m mailbox	v vegetable garden
e entrance sign	n neighbor	w welcome sign
f fence	o outdoors	x children x-ing (children
g garden	p park	crossing sign)
h house	q quiet zone	y yard
i ice cream truck	r recycle bins	z petting zoo

WHAT TO DO

1. Read the children one of the neighborhood books (listed to the left). Talk with the children about the different neighborhood words. Explain that they will be learning some new words that neighbors use in their neighborhoods.
2. Show the children the alphabet chart. Recite the alphabet with the children and explain all the unfamiliar words on the chart. Demonstrate for the children how to find the first letter of each word, and then how to find the matching letter card.
3. Ask a child to choose a word from the chart and name the letter. Ask the child to choose a friend to find the matching letter card. Point out the first letter of the word and discuss how the shape of the letter matches: straight lines, curved lines, and so on. Continue as long as the children are interested.

ASSESSMENT

To assess the children's learning, consider the following:
● Can the children recognize letters of the alphabet?
● Can the children recite the alphabet?
● Can the children point to the first letter of a word?

Children's Books

A Chair for My Mother
by Vera Williams
*Jobs Around My
Neighborhood* by
Gladys Rosa-Mendoza
*Franklin's
Neighborhood* by
Paulette Bourgeois
Qunito's Neighborhood
by Ina Cumpiano
*Who Are the People in
Your Neighborhood?* by
Naomi Kleinberg

Susan Oldham Hill, Lakeland, FL

Spell the Store Name

4+

LEARNING OBJECTIVES

The children will:
1. Begin to recognize and name letters.
2. Put letters in the correct order to spell known words.

Materials

digital camera
computer
printer
card stock paper
scissors (adult use
    only)
laminator

VOCABULARY

order   sign   spell   store

PREPARATION

● Ask children's parents and family member for permission to take the children on a neighborhood walk.
● Ask parents and family members to volunteer to accompany the children on the field trip.

WHAT TO DO

1. Take the children (and your camera) on a walk around the neighborhood.
2. As you walk, point out the various stores and talk about the things they sell there.
3. Take a picture of each store sign. Make sure to zoom in closely so you get a clear shot of the sign's letters.
4. Back at the center, upload the pictures to a computer and crop them to remove any extra background images. You want to have a close-up image of just the letters on the sign.
5. Print the pictures in a large size, for example 6" x 8" or larger. Make two copies of each picture and laminate them.
6. Cut one of the pictures of each pair apart into its individual letters.
7. Make a matching game by giving the children an uncut picture and the cut up letters. They can match the letters to the ones on the picture.
8. After the children have some experience with the game, challenge them to put the letters in the correct order without using the picture guide.
9. Make comments as the children work. For example, you can ask them to recall the name of the store in the picture, or ask them to say the names and letter sounds of the individual letters.

ASSESSMENT

To assess the children's learning, consider the following:
● Are the children able to match the cut letters to those in the uncut pictures?
● Can the children identify the letters by name?

Children's Books

Curious George Visits a Toy Store by Margret Rey, H. A. Rey, and Martha Weston
Grandpa's Corner Store by DyAnne DiSalvo
Mama and Papa Have a Store by Amelia Lau Carling
Signs at the Store by Mary Hill

Virginia Jean Herrod, Columbia, SC

"A" Is for Alaska

5+

LEARNING OBJECTIVES

The children will:
1. Learn about different geographical locations.
2. Develop their familiarity with the alphabet.

Materials

5–6 globes (or world maps)

VOCABULARY

alphabet	countries	globe
home	letters	world

WHAT TO DO

1. Begin by discussing the world with the children. Talk about how there are many countries. Ask the children if any of them or their families are from different countries.
2. Divide the children into several groups. Give each group a globe. Talk about how globes are models of the world. Show the children how the globes have various different countries on them. Point out the United States, as well as some of the countries from which the children's families originated.
3. Tell the children they will be doing a letter search on their globes. Name a letter of the alphabet. Ask each group of children to look all over the globe for a place (country, city, ocean, or continent) that starts with that letter.
4. After all the groups find a word that starts with that letter, invite each group to share their location. Help the children say the words they find.
5. The other groups then seek out those locations on their globes as well.
6. Name another letter and continue the game through several letters of the alphabet.

TEACHER-TO-TEACHER TIP

- If time allows, search the internet to provide information about the locations that the children name in this activity.

Children's Books

Alaska ABC Book by Charlene Kreeger
Alphabet City by Stephen T. Johnson
The Alphabet Tree by Leo Lionni
Away from Home by Anita Lobel

ASSESSMENT

To assess the children's learning, consider the following:
- Do the children understand that the globe is a model of the planet Earth?
- Can the children locate the United States on the globe?
- Can the children locate words on the globe that start with particular letters?

Shyamala Shanmugasundaram, Navi Mumbai, India

ABC America!

5+

LEARNING OBJECTIVES

The children will:
1. Develop their understanding of alphabetical order.
2. Match initial letters to words.
3. Develop their understanding of maps.

Materials

alphabet cards
picture-word cards
 with state
 outlines and their
 names
map of the United
 States

VOCABULARY

after   alphabet   before   order   state   state names

WHAT TO DO

1. Introduce the activity by reciting the alphabet with the children. Show the children the alphabet cards, explaining the letters.
2. Show the children a map of the United States. Talk with the children about how the country is made up of states, and how each state has a name. Ask the children if they know the name of the state they live in. Challenge the children to locate their state on the map.
3. Set out eight alphabet cards and eight state cards so the children can see all of them at once. (For younger or less-experienced children, set out only two cards from each group.) Be sure the letter cards include the first letters of the states on display.
4. Challenge the children to identify the state names, and to match the alphabet cards to states whose names begin with those letters.
5. Consider asking the children to try putting the state cards in correct alphabetical order.

ASSESSMENT

To assess the children's learning, consider the following:
- Can the children identify the letters by name?
- Can the children identify the states by name?
- Can the children match the correct alphabet letters to the state cards?
- Can the children put the state cards in alphabetical order?

Susan Oldham Hill, Lakeland, FL

Children's Books

The Absolutely Awful Alphabet by Mordicai Gerstein
Alphabet City by Stephen Johnson
The Alphabet Tree by Leo Lionni
From Acorn to Zoo: and Everything in Between in Alphabetical Order by Satoshi Kitamura

I Wish I Could Visit...

5+

LEARNING OBJECTIVES

The children will:
1. Think of a state they would like to visit.
2. Develop their oral language expression.
3. Begin to identify letters.
4. Express creativity through illustration.

Materials

white paper
crayons and
   markers
hole punch
yarn or silver rings

VOCABULARY

community   country   home   illustrate   state   visit

WHAT TO DO

1. Gather the children together and read books about the states, including the children's home state (see list to the left for suggestions).
2. Provide each child with paper, markers, and crayons.
3. Ask each child to think of a state he or she would like to visit. Then have each child finish the following sentence by naming that state: "I wish I could visit _____."
4. Write their answers on their papers, and say each letter aloud while writing it. Encourage the children to name the letters with you.
5. Have the children illustrate their ideas.
6. Punch holes in the papers and bind them together with yarn or silver rings to make a book for the classroom library.

POEM

I Wish I Could by Laura Wynkoop
I wish I could sit on the seashore in Oregon,
And see maple trees in Vermont.
I wish I could travel all over the country
And go anywhere that I want.

ASSESSMENT

To assess the children's learning, consider the following:
- Can the children name single states they want to visit, and explain why they chose them?
- Can the children name the letters in the states they chose?

Laura Wynkoop, San Dimas, CA

Children's Books

A Is for America by Devin Scillian
America the Beautiful by Katharine Lee Bates and Neil Waldman
If America Were a Village by David J. Smith
The Scrambled States of America by Laurie Keller
The United States by Robin S. Doak
Wee Sing America by Pamela Conn Beall

Neighborhood Clues

5+

LEARNING OBJECTIVES

The children will:

1. Learn about people and professions that help their community.
2. Name occupations based on clues.

Materials

bag or box
cards
marker
pictures of
  neighborhood
  workers: mail
  carrier, lawn care
  worker, meter
  reader, pest
  control worker,
  newspaper
  carrier, ice cream
  truck driver,
  delivery worker,
  sanitation worker

VOCABULARY

delivery worker   ice cream truck driver   lawn care worker
mail carrier   newspaper carrier   pest control worker
sanitation worker

PREPARATION

- Write the following clues on cards:
  - When your grass grows too tall, I come to trim it down.
  - I come whenever you have too many ants and roaches in your kitchen.
  - I come every week to take away your garbage.
  - I come early in the morning and leave something on the driveway for you to read later.
  - When someone sends you a letter, I'm the one who comes to your house every day to bring it to you.
  - You always know when I'm coming with my refrigerated truck, because you can hear my music playing.

WHAT TO DO

1. Show the children the pictures of neighborhood workers and discuss how these people help the community. Ask the children how many neighborhood workers they have seen in their neighborhoods.
2. Ask a child to draw a card out of the bag. Read the clue to the children, and challenge them to guess which community helper it describes.

ASSESSMENT

To assess the children's learning, consider the following:

- Can the children identify the jobs in the pictures?
- Can the children guess the jobs the clues describe?

Susan Oldham Hill , Lakeland, FL

Children's Books

Delivering Your Mail by Ann Owen
Jobs Around My Neighborhood by Gladys Rosa-Mendoza
Louie's Search by Ezra Jack Keats
Who Are the People in Your Neighborhood? by Naomi Kleinberg

An Igloo for My Home

LEARNING OBJECTIVES

The children will:
1. Develop their large motor skills.
2. Practice their social skills.
3. Learn about building an igloo.

Materials

3 or more large boxes or crates

3 or more white sheets

VOCABULARY

Alaska	cold	Eskimo	home
ice	igloo	Inuit	wilderness

WHAT TO DO

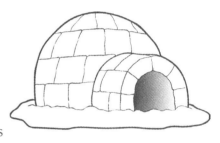

1. Gather the children together and read them a book about igloos.
2. Ask the children if they know what an igloo is. Show the children the pictures in the books. Explain that some, but not all, of the Eskimo people used to live in igloos and some still do.
3. Talk about living in a house made of ice. Ask the children if they think it would be cold inside an igloo, and whether the ice would keep them warm.
4. Help the children build their own "igloo." Spread out the crates, leaving a center area for the inside of the igloo.
5. Put the sheets over the crates. If there are enough crates, stack them, safely, two high. Make sure they will not fall on the children.
6. Leave a "doorway" for an entrance. Have the children enter the igloo two or three at a time. When they leave, they each invite another child to go into the igloo.

TEACHER-TO-TEACHER TIP

● If it is cold weather when doing this activity, have the children put on their coats before going into the igloo. When they get inside, they take off their coats, until they leave again.

ASSESSMENT

To assess the children's learning, consider the following:
● What can the children say about igloos?
● Do the children think they could stay warm in an igloo?
● Do the children understand why the Eskimos had to build igloos for homes?

Children's Books

Building an Igloo by Ulli Steltzer
The Igloo by Charlotte and David Yue
Igloo Makeover by Club Penguin
Look Inside an Igloo by Mari Schuh

Shirley Anne Ramaley, Sun City, AZ

Living in a City

4+

The children will:
1. Learn about living in cities.
2. Learn to cooperate and develop social skills.
3. Develop their small and large motor skills.

Materials

interlocking blocks
  and other types
  of blocks
small figurines of
  people, dogs,
  and other "city
  dwellers"

VOCABULARY

city	cooperate	friend	help
house	people	street	town

WHAT TO DO

1. Talk with the children about the kinds of environments where people live. Talk about cities, suburbs, small towns, rural areas, and so on. Ask the children how they would describe the place they live in. Tell the children that in cities, many people live close together.
2. Show the children the materials. Pair the children together, and invite the pairs to work together to make buildings.
3. After the children finish building, invite them to come together and make one city neighborhood out of their buildings. Talk with the children about how they will have to cooperate to make everything fit together.

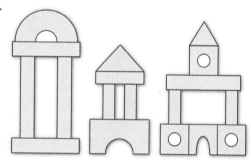

ASSESSMENT

To assess the children's learning, consider the following:
- Do the children understand the differences between various residential environments?
- Are the children able to work together to build individual structures and organize them into a city?

Shirley Anne Ramaley, Sun City, AZ

Children's Books

Living in a City by Lisa
Trumbauer and Gail
Saunders-Smith
*Living in Suburban
Communities* by Kristin
Sterling
Living in a Small Town
by Lisa Trumbauer and
Gail Saunders-Smith
Living in Cities by Neil
Morris
Sleepless in LazyTown
by Magnus Scheving
and Artful Doodlers

Pack Your Clothing

LEARNING OBJECTIVES

The children will:
1. Learn about the different kinds of clothes appropriate for different climates.
2. Learn about different states.
3. Develop their counting skills.

Materials

2 large, empty suitcases
various clothing items appropriate for very hot and very cold climates

VOCABULARY

boots	clothes	cold	gloves	hot
shorts	sweater	swimming suit	warm	

PREPARATION

- Ask every child to bring a warm- or cold-weather clothing item from home.
- Tag every clothing item with the name of the child who brought it in to class.
- Write "Alaska" and "Hawai'i" on cards, and place one card inside each suitcase.

WHAT TO DO

1. Talk with the children about how the weather can be very different in different places. Some climates are warm while others are cold.
2. Show the children the two suitcases. Tell the children they are going to help pack the suitcases for two different places, one to cold-weather Alaska and one to warm-weather Hawai'i.
3. Invite the children to take turns picking up an item of clothing, identifying it by name, saying whether it is for cold or warm weather, and putting it in the appropriate suitcase. Encourage the children to help one another in the decision-making process.
4. When the activity is done, challenge the children to count the number of items in each suitcase.
5. Leave the suitcases and clothing out so the children can explore them further.

TEACHER-TO-TEACHER TIP

- Consider extending the activity by having the children sort the clothing items by color.

ASSESSMENT

To assess the children's learning, consider the following:
- Can the children identify the different clothing items?
- Can the children say whether the clothing is for warm or cool climates?

Shyamala Shanmugasundaram, Navi Mumbai, India

Children's Books

Clothes by Debbie Bailey
The Jacket I Wear in the Snow by Shirley Neitzel
Joseph Had a Little Overcoat by Simms Taback

Profession Puzzles

4+

LEARNING OBJECTIVES

The children will:
1. Learn to identify the clothes worn by various professionals.
2. Develop their interpersonal skills.
3. Develop their small motor skills.

Materials

card stock
scissors (adult use only)
glue
matching large and small images of various professionals
laminating materials (optional)

VOCABULARY

above	below	beside	construction worker	doctor
firefighter	mail carrier	next to	police officer	under

PREPARATION

- Glue onto card stock the large pictures of various professionals (construction worker, doctor, firefighter, mail carrier, police officer, and so on). Do the same with the smaller, matching pictures.
- Laminate all the pictures. Cut the large pictures into several puzzle pieces.

WHAT TO DO

1. Display the small pictures of the various professionals, and ask the children to identify them.
2. Show the children the larger pictures cut into puzzle pieces.
3. Pair the children together and have them take turns putting the profession pictures together, referring to the small, uncut pictures if they need help. Encourage the children to use positional words to help one another describe where the various puzzle pieces belong.

Children's Books

Monkey with a Tool Belt by Chris Monroe
The Toolbox by Anne Rockwell
Tools by Taro Miura
Tools by Holly Mann

ASSESSMENT

To assess the children's learning, consider the following:
- Can the children identify the names of the professions in the pictures?
- Can the children work together to put the profession puzzles together correctly?

Jackie Wright, Enid, OK

Special Delivering

LEARNING OBJECTIVES

The children will:
1. Create mail for each other.
2. Sort and deliver class mail.
3. Understand the role of the mail carrier.

Materials

sample mail
crayons
box with a slit cut
   in the top
stamps
paper
items to identify
   each table, or
   "address," such
   as colored star
   stickers
picture of each
   student with a
   paper clip
   attached

VOCABULARY

address	deliver	mail	mail carrier
mailbox	return address	sort	stamp

PREPARATION

- Set up a classroom post office equipped with the materials in the list to the left. Add the job of mail carrier to your list of class jobs.

WHAT TO DO

1. Show the children several sample pieces of mail.
2. Ask the children if they can identify the address, return address, and stamp on the mail. Help the children if necessary.
3. Discuss mail carriers and the process of mail delivery.
4. Tell the children they will create and deliver class mail.
5. Have the children make pictures for specific classmates and bring completed pictures to the post office.
6. Help the children fold, stamp, and "address" their mail by adding the picture of the child and table identifier. The return address is the name of the sender with a table identifier.
7. As a group, sort the mail by address. Assign your first mail carrier. Then deliver the mail and collect the pictures of the children for future use.
8. Allow several times each week for the class to make letters and for mail delivery. Remind them to include both the "address" and a stamp.

TEACHER-TO-TEACHER TIP

- You can use stickers for stamps.

ASSESSMENT

To assess the children's learning, consider the following:
- Do the children understand the basic function mail serves?
- Can the children explain how mail is sent and delivered?
- Can the children say who performs this task in the community?

Children's Books

Mail Carriers at Work
by Karen Latchana
Kenney
Millie Waits for the Mail
by Alexander
Steffensmeier
The Post Office Book by
Gail Gibbons

Debbie Vilardi, Commack, NY

The Dentist

4+

The children will:
1. Learn about the important role that dentists play in the community.
2. Develop their basic counting skills.

Materials

crayons or markers
blank index cards
magazines
newspaper
glue
paper plates

VOCABULARY

brush	care	dentist
floss	numbers 1–20	teeth

PREPARATION

- Cut 20 cards in the shapes of teeth, or draw tooth outlines on several individual cards.
- Write a number from 1–20 on each individual card. (Alternatively, write the numbers one to five on four sets of individual cards.)
- Cut out many small squares to serve as teeth.

WHAT TO DO

1. Begin by talking with the children about their teeth. Discuss how important their teeth are, what they use them for, and so on.
2. Ask the children if they have ever been to the dentist. Explain that the dentist is an important member of the community.

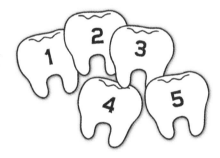

3. Show the children the large numbered tooth cutouts. Explain that most children between the ages of three and five have 20 teeth.
4. Count the large individual tooth cutouts aloud for the children, challenging the children to count along.
5. Set out the large numbered tooth cutouts as well as the small cutout tooth squares.
6. Challenge the children to place the corresponding number of tooth squares on the large numbered tooth cutouts.

ASSESSMENT

To assess the children's learning, consider the following:
- Do the children know what a dentist does?
- Can the children place the correct number of tooth squares on the numbered tooth cutouts?

Cookie Zingarelli, Columbus, OH

Children's Books

Andrew's Loose Tooth by Roberta Munsch
The Berenstain Bears Visit the Dentist by Stan Berenstain
The Tooth Book by Dr. Seuss
Franklin and the Tooth Fairy by Paulette Bourgeois & Brenda Clark
No Tooth, No Quarter by Jan Buller & Susan Schade

How Many People Live in Your House?

Materials

20 large wooden
blocks
marker
masking tape

LEARNING OBJECTIVES

The children will:
1. Begin to identify numerals.
2. Develop their counting ability and understanding of one-to-one correspondence.

VOCABULARY

beat   count   house   number   tap

PREPARATION

- Write the numbers from 1–10 on a piece of masking tape. Attach each number to the bottom of a block.
- Display the assorted blocks in a group (number side down) in the center of the circle time area, to represent a small city or village of homes.

WHAT TO DO

1. Gather 10 children together and talk about different-sized families, and other living arrangements.
2. Give each child an unnumbered block and invite the children to look at the small block "homes."
3. Tell the children that a different number of people live in each of the "homes," and that number is on the bottom of each block.
4. Ask each child to take one "home" and then return to the circle.
5. Tell the children to look at the numbers on the bottoms of their "homes."
6. Ask the children to pick up their unnumbered blocks and separate into groups of two. Rather than tell their partners how many people live in their homes, ask the children to tap the blocks together the correct number of times.
7. Help children who are having trouble determining the correct number of times to tap their blocks together.
8. When the children finish, ask them to return their block homes to their original locations.

ASSESSMENT

To assess the children's learning, consider the following:
- Can the children say how many people live in their homes?
- Can the children identify the numbers on the bottoms of their block homes?

Children's Books

All Families Are Special by Norma Simon
All Kinds of Families by Mary Ann Hoberman
The Family Book by Todd Parr
Houses and Homes by Ann Morris
Homes by Nicola Baxter

Mary J. Murray, Mazomanie, WI

Look and See, Lift and Count

4+

6 shoeboxes
6 sets of plastic toy
people, or 6
pictures of
people in family
groups
pictures of 6
different types of
homes from
various cultures
and countries

LEARNING OBJECTIVES

The children will:
1. Become familiar with various types of homes in different cultures.
2. Improve their counting skills.
3. Appreciate different cultures.

VOCABULARY

adobe	dwelling	house	igloo
log cabin	teepee	trailer	yurt

PREPARATION

- Attach one picture to the outside bottom side of each shoebox.
- Set each box on a table upside down, with the picture facing up.
- Place a set of people toys or a picture of a family underneath each shoebox.

WHAT TO DO

1. Talk with the children about where they live. Ask them to describe particular features of their homes. Ask the children if they have ever seen a different kind of home. Explain that people in other parts of the country and the world live in homes that are different from those in which the children live.
2. Show the children pictures of dwellings from other areas of the country or world. Explain where each one comes from, and identify its various features. Ask the children to point out ways in which the homes are similar to or different from their homes.
3. Tell the children that each shoebox home has a different number of people living in it. Lift each box and show the children the people that live inside that home.
4. Set out the materials and invite the children to explore and imagine the lives of the people in the different homes. Challenge the children to count the number of people living in the different homes.

ASSESSMENT

To assess the children's learning, consider the following:
- Can the children count the number of people in each shoebox home?
- Can the children describe the similarities and differences among the homes on display?

Mary J. Murray, Mazomanie, WI

Children's Books

City and Country Homes by Debbie Gallagher
Homes in Many Cultures by Heather Adamson
Mud, Grass, and Ice Homes by Debbie Gallagher

On Preschool Street

LEARNING OBJECTIVES

The children will:
1. Begin to identify the numbers 1–10.
2. Practice putting numbers in order.
3. Develop their awareness of street names and house numbers.

Materials

colored
  construction
  paper
scissors (adult use
  only)
marker
images or
  construction-
  paper outlines of
  houses

VOCABULARY

address   home   house
location   number   street

PREPARATION

- On one sheet of paper, write "Preschool Street" so that it resembles a street sign.
- Number the various house pictures or outlines from 1–10.
- Set out the "Preschool Street" sign and put the house pictures or outlines out in a random order.

WHAT TO DO

1. Begin by talking with the children about where they live. Ask them if they know their addresses or know their apartment numbers.
2. Talk with the children about the importance of addresses, explaining they are how people find specific locations.
3. Show the children the houses on "Preschool Street." Say each number with the children. Ask the children if there is something odd about the number. Explain that the numbers are out of order, and that addresses need to be in order to be useful.
4. Challenge the children to put the houses in the correct order.
   Note: Consider providing a correctly ordered list of numbers the children can refer to if they have trouble putting the numbers in order.

TEACHER-TO-TEACHER TIP

- For more advanced children, try using addresses that have two or three numbers in them.

ASSESSMENT

To assess the children's learning, consider the following:
- Can the children identify the numbers on the houses?
- Can the children order the numbers from 1–10?
- Do the children understand the function of addresses?

Mary J. Murray, Mazomanie, WI

Children's Books

Homes by Fiona
  Macdonald
Houses by Lynn M.
  Stone
Houses and Homes by
  Ann Morris
Where Is My Home? by
  Robin Nelson

Telephone Number

4

LEARNING OBJECTIVES

The children will:
1. Familiarize themselves with the numbers zero to nine.
2. Begin to memorize their phone numbers.

Materials

large piece of cardboard or construction paper
markers
scissors (adult use only)

VOCABULARY

call	dial	home
numbers 0–9	telephone	

PREPARATION

- Cut the outline of a large phone out of the cardboard.
- Cut one small outline of a phone for each child.
- Write the numbers zero to nine, as written on a phone, on the large and small phone cutouts.
- Collect the children's home phone numbers from the children's families prior to this activity.
- Write each child's name and number on one phone cutout.

WHAT TO DO

1. Talk with the children about telephones. Ask the children about who they have talked to on the phone. Explain why it is important that all the children know their phone numbers.
2. Show the children the large and small phone cutouts. Give the children their individualized phones. Help them read their numbers at the top.
3. Sing the following song with the children. Recite your phone number, hitting the buttons on the large phone to reinforce the connection. Encourage the children to do the same on their small phone cutouts as they sing:

Phone Number by Kristen Peters
(Tune to "Oh, My Darling")
There are ten numbers, there are ten numbers,
There are ten numbers to call my home.
xxx-xxx-xxxx (children recite their phone numbers)
Are the numbers for my phone.

ASSESSMENT

To assess the children's learning, consider the following:
- Can the children recite their phone numbers?
- Can the children touch the correct numbers on their phone cutouts as they say their phone numbers?
- Can the children explain why it is important to know their phone numbers?

Children's Books

Hello, Hello by Fumiko Takeshita
Manners on the Phone by Carrie Finn
Teatime Piglet by Steve Bland
Telephones by Kristin Petrie

Kristen Peters, Mattituck, NY

U.S. Symbol Patterns

4+

LEARNING OBJECTIVES

The children will:
1. Identify important symbols of the United States.
2. Develop an understanding of ABAB patterns.
3. Develop their small motor skills.

Materials

several sets of pictures of American symbols, such as a bald eagle, the American flag, George Washington, the Liberty Bell, and so on

VOCABULARY

America	bald eagle	flag	George Washington
Liberty Bell	map	symbol	United States

WHAT TO DO

1. Talk with the children about the United States. Ask the children if they can think of images that remind them of the United States.
2. Show the children the pictures of American symbols. Explain their importance to the United States.
3. Put two of the images in an ABAB pattern, and have the children identify the pictures.
4. Give the pictures to the children and encourage them to copy the pattern.
5. After the children complete the pattern, make a new pattern for the children to copy. Continue this through several patterns. Consider letting the children make patterns for one another to match.

ASSESSMENT

To assess the children's learning, consider the following:
- Can the children name the symbols?
- Can the children copy ABAB and other patterns?

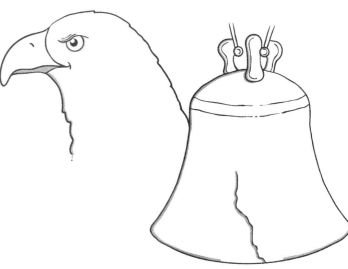

Children's Books

A Is for America by Devin Scillian
America the Beautiful by Katharine Bates
The Pledge of Allegiance by Francis Bellamy
Wee Sing America by Pamela Conn Beall

Jackie Wright, Enid, OK

Neighborhood Store

5+

LEARNING OBJECTIVES

The children will:
1. Familiarize themselves with coins.
2. Develop their ability to count from zero to nine.

Materials

markers
blank stickers
cans and boxes of
    vegetables,
    macaroni, and
    similar grocery
    items
price tags
coins
box for coins

VOCABULARY

cents	dime	money
nickel	penny	quarter

PREPARATION

● Make price tags and attach them to the grocery items.

WHAT TO DO

1. Talk with the children about trips they have taken to local grocery and convenience stores. Ask the children what they did while they were there, and what they left the store with. Talk about how these stores provide food, groceries, and other necessary items.
2. Display one of the priced grocery items. Read the number on the price tag and explain how this indicates how much the item costs. Explain that a nickel is the same as five pennies, and a dime equals 10 pennies.
3. Give each of the children some coins and invite them to shop and "buy" some items. Show the children how to check the price tags, challenging them to identify the numerals on the tags, and then count out enough coins to pay.
4. Select a few children to be cashiers, and help them count out change for the children who make the purchases.

TEACHER-TO-TEACHER TIP

● Using real coins provides a more realistic sense of how to use money.

ASSESSMENT

To assess the children's learning, consider the following:
● Can the children recognize the names of coins?
● Can the children recognize the sign for cents?
● Can the children recognize the numerals from zero to nine?
● Can the children count out the correct number of coins?

Susan Oldham Hill, Lakeland, FL

Children's Books

All About Money by Erin Roberson
Everybody Brings Noodles by Norah Dooley
Grandpa's Corner Store by DyAnne DiSalvo
Money (DK Eyewitness Books) by Joe Cribb

Open the Door

5+

LEARNING OBJECTIVES

The children will:
1. Explore the differences between houses and apartment buildings.
2. Improve their counting skills.
3. Begin to identify numbers.

Materials

colored card stock
markers
scissors (adult use
only)

VOCABULARY

apartment building	count	families
house	number	people

PREPARATION

* Cut out several house shapes. Mark each one with a separate number from 1–10.
* On several uncut sheets of paper, make an apartment building by drawing a vertical line down the center, then three horizontal lines to make eight equal rectangles. Mark each rectangle with a number from one to eight.

WHAT TO DO

1. Engage the children in a conversation about where they all live. Do they live in houses? Apartments? With the children, count how many of them live in each type of home. Compare the numbers.
2. Show the children the different cutouts of houses and apartments. Explain that different numbers of people live in all the different locations, and that the numbers on the apartments and houses indicate the number of inhabitants.
3. Challenge the children to identify the numbers on the houses and apartments. Invite the children to make up stories about the families that live in the various houses and apartments.

TEACHER-TO-TEACHER TIP

* For more advanced children, consider challenging them to add up the number of inhabitants who live on a single floor of one of the apartments, or to add up the total number of people who live in more than one of the houses.

Children's Books

City Homes by Nicola Barber
Houses and Homes by Ann Morris
Let's Go Home by Cynthia Rylant
This Is My House by Arthur Dorros

ASSESSMENT

To assess the children's learning, consider the following:
* Can the children explain the differences between apartment buildings, and houses?
* Can the children identify the numbers of inhabitants in each house and apartment?

Mary J. Murray, Mazomanie, WI

Populations

5+

LEARNING OBJECTIVES

The children will:
1. Identify and learn about numbers.
2. Become familiar with the word "population."
3. Learn the names of nearby cities.

Materials

drawing paper
markers
dry-erase boards or
   paper

VOCABULARY

city	less	more
number	people	population

PREPARATION

- Find out the population of the local city or town, as well as five or six more nearby cities, towns, or villages. Select city names with which children may be familiar.
- Print each city name and its population in large letters on a sheet of drawing paper.

WHAT TO DO

1. Engage the children in a discussion about the area where they live. Talk about how when you count the people who live in a place the term for this is "population." Display the sheet of paper that lists the local city or town and its population.
2. Recite the number aloud and ask the children to repeat it. Explain that they themselves make up part of this population number.
3. Set out dry-erase boards or paper and markers and invite the children to write the number on their dry-erase board or on the paper.
4. Select individual children to stand up and recite the big number again, then have them erase the number.
5. Display another paper with a city name and its population and recite it aloud. Invite the children to recite the number and city name aloud, and then write it on their dry erase board or paper.
6. Continue until the children explore writing and saying the populations of all the selected local cities, towns, and villages.

ASSESSMENT

To assess the children's learning, consider the following:
- Are children able to repeat each city name?
- Can children repeat each number aloud?
- Can the children explain what "population" means?

Mary J. Murray, Mazomanie, WI

Children's Books

I Live in the City by Gini Holland
I Live in a Town by Gini Holland
People by Peter Spier
Richard Scarry's What Do People Do All Day by Richard Scarry

Road Trip

5+

LEARNING OBJECTIVES

The children will:
1. Identify local cities by name.
2. Explore comparing distances.

Materials

small toy cars
blocks
5 sheets of 8" x 11"
    colored paper
marker
masking tape
plain paper

VOCABULARY

car   city names   drive   far   near   road   travel

PREPARATION

- Write the names of five local cities or towns on sheets of paper.
- Set the sheets of paper on the classroom floor in a way that loosely matches those cities' and towns' locations in relation to one another.
- Use masking tape to create "roads" joining the cities to one another.
- Set assorted blocks in each "city" to represent buildings.
- On separate sheets of paper, write the distances between each city and set them out on the floor map.

WHAT TO DO

1. Show the children the floor map of the local area and surrounding cities or villages, reading the place names aloud. Ask the children if they have ever been to any of those places.
2. Point out how some locations are near and others are farther away. Read each distance card aloud.
3. Invite the children to drive toy cars from one city to another. Discuss the distances with the children, talking about which cities are near and which are far away.
4. Encourage the children to make up stories as they move the cars on the map.

ASSESSMENT

To assess the children's learning, consider the following:
- Can the children say which locations are nearer and which are farther away from a particular place?
- Can the children say the names of the locations?

Mary J. Murray, Mazomanie, WI

Children's Books

Map Basics by Maxwell Baber
Map Mania by Michael Dispzio
You Are Here by Jennifer Blizin Gillis

State Birds and More Birds 5+

LEARNING OBJECTIVES

The children will:
1. Learn about state birds.
2. Develop their counting and patterning skills.

VOCABULARY

beak	bird	color	eat	feathers	feeder
fly	food	head	tail	wings	

WHAT TO DO

1. Explain to the children that each state has a special bird they call their "state bird."
2. Show the children pictures of the local state bird and provide the children with some information about the bird. Ask the children to describe the bird and identify its colors, as well as its beak, wings, feathers, and claws.
3. Display the pictures of other birds that are common in the local area.
4. Create a pattern with the pictures of the birds. Challenge the children to identify which bird is their state bird.
5. Provide the children with copies of the pictures of the various birds, and invite them to match the pattern of birds, as well as make their own patterns.

TEACHER-TO-TEACHER TIP
- Consider having the children match the states to their state birds.

ASSESSMENT
To assess the children's learning, consider the following:
- Can the children name their state bird?
- Can the children identify the state bird?
- Can the children match a pattern of bird pictures?

Mary J. Murray, Mazomanie, WI

Children's Books

Bird and Flower Emblems of the United States by Hilda Simon
Birds, Nests, and Eggs by Mel Boring
Feathers for Lunch by Lois Ehlert
State Birds by Arthur Singer
United Tweets of America by Hudson Talbott

State Map Math

5+

LEARNING OBJECTIVES

The children will:

1. Learn about U.S. states.
2. Become familiar with reading maps.
3. Develop their math skills.

Materials

large wall map of
the United States
small sticky notes
or dot stickers

VOCABULARY

far	friend	home	location
near	relative	state	state names

WHAT TO DO

1. Show the children the map. Talk about how maps are small versions of large locations, and that this map shows the United States.
2. Challenge the children to point out their home state.
3. Ask the children if they have friends or relatives who live in other states. Ask the children to name those states, and to try and point them out on the map.
4. Put a small sticker on each state for every friend or relative the children have living in those locations.
5. Ask the children if those states are close to or far from their home state.
6. Count the number of states between the children's home state and the various states where their friends and relatives live.
7. With the children, count the numbers of dots they put on the map, and compare the numbers of friends and relatives living in different states. Ask the children which state has the largest number of dots, and which has the smallest number of dots.

ASSESSMENT

To assess the children's learning, consider the following:

- Can the children locate and name their home state as well as other states?
- Can the children identify states where friends and relatives live?
- Are the children able to compare the numbers of friends and relatives living in the various states?

Sarah Stasik, Bent Mountain, VA

Children's Books

As the Crow Flies by Gail Hartman
Maps and Globes by Jack Knowlton
Me on the Map by Joan Sweeney
There's a Map on My Lap! by Tish Rabe

What I Want to Be...

5+

LEARNING OBJECTIVES

The children will:
1. Learn about jobs they can do when they grow up.
2. Develop their math and graphing skills.

Materials

pictures of
  community
  workers
large sheet of
  construction
  paper
sticky notes
pencils or markers

VOCABULARY

career	choose	compare	graph
job	occupation	unique	vote

PREPARATION
- Create a simple graph titled "What I Want to Be," with pictures of different occupations along the base of the graph. Also add an "other" column.
- Write each child's name on a sticky note.

WHAT TO DO
1. Gather the children and show them the graph. Review each of the chosen jobs represented on the graph, discussing the children's experience of each career.
2. Ask the children to take turns attaching the sticky notes with their names on them to the columns of the careers they would most like to pursue when they grow up.
3. Invite the children who put their sticky notes in the "other" column to describe the careers they want to pursue when they grow up.
4. After the children add their sticky notes to the graph, talk with the children about the results. Count the number of sticky notes in each column. Ask the children which career most of them want to pursue. Ask them which career seems the most unusual.
5. Set the graph up in the classroom for the children to show and discuss with their parents and family members later.

ASSESSMENT
To assess the children's learning, consider the following:
- Can the children name the workers and describe some of the jobs they do?
- Can the children read the graph to see which career was the most popular?

Shelley Hoster, Norcross, GA

Children's Books

Career Day by Anne Rockwell
When I Grow Up by P.K. Hallinan
Whose Hat Is This? by Katz Cooper

Good Morning, Neighbor 3+

LEARNING OBJECTIVES

The children will:
1. Recite a rhyme to other children.
2. Develop their social skills.

Materials

VOCABULARY

community   greeting   hello   morning   neighbor   polite

WHAT TO DO

1. Ask the children about their experience leaving their homes that morning. Did they see any neighbors when they left? Did they say hello to their neighbors? Tell the children it is a nice and normal thing to greet their neighbors, who are a part of their community.

2. Teach the children the following greeting song as a way to encourage them to greet their neighbors when they see them:

Good Morning, Neighbor! by Susan Oldham Hill
(Tune: "You Are My Sunshine")
Good morning, Neighbor! I'm glad to see you,
And to know that you're my friend!
It's good to meet you; I'm glad to greet you!
Good morning, Neighbor! Good morning, again!

TEACHER-TO-TEACHER TIP

● In future days, consider inviting children to recite this song to one another as they come into the classroom at the beginning of the day.

ASSESSMENT

To assess the children's learning, consider the following:
● Do the children understand who their neighbors are?
● Do the children enjoy greeting their classmate friends and neighbors?

Susan Oldham Hill, Lakeland, FL

Children's Books

Everybody Cooks Rice by Norah Dooley
Jobs Around My Neighborhood by Gladys Rosa-Mendoza
Who Are the People in Your Neighborhood? by Naomi Keinberg

Moving Time

5+

LEARNING OBJECTIVES

The children will:
1. Identify city names.
2. Count house shapes.
3. Improve their large motor skills.

Materials

sidewalk chalk

VOCABULARY

cities   count   houses   move   numbers   streets

PREPARATION

- Draw three groups of house shapes on the playground area using the sidewalk chalk. Leave 20' or more of space between each city (group of houses).
- Write each city name near each group of houses.
- Draw one house per child.

WHAT TO DO

1. Invite the children outdoors for this fun movement activity.
2. Gather the children around the chalk drawings.
3. Explain that there are three cities. Recite the city names aloud. Ask the children if they have ever lived in different cities or towns, and why they moved.
4. Ask the children to count the houses in each city as they step into each house shape.
5. After the children are familiar with the locations, invite each child to pick one house in which to stand.
6. Call out, "Move into a new house!" At that command, the children run or walk to a new house. Children may choose to move to different cities or stay in the cities they are in. If children move to new cities, ask them to name the cities they moved to, as well as the names of the cities they left.
7. Repeat the activity as children have fun running and stepping from house to house and city to city on the playground.

ASSESSMENT

To assess the children's learning, consider the following:
- Do the children know the names of the cities?
- Can the children count the number of cities, houses, and houses within a particular city?

Mary J. Murray, Mazomanie, WI

Children's Books

Mitchell Is Moving by Marjorie Weinman Sharmat
Moving Day by Cyndy Szekeres
Moving House by Anne Civardi
We're Moving by Heather Maisner

Building My Town

5

LEARNING OBJECTIVES

The children will:

1. Make buildings with boxes, cartons, and bags.
2. Develop their problem-solving and interpersonal skills.
3. Develop their large and small motor skills.

Materials

photos of towns
and cities
blocks
various types of
boxes
lunch bags
clean milk and
juice cartons
paper
markers
construction paper
child-safe scissors
tape
string
yarn
glue

VOCABULARY

building	gas station	house	library	park
post office	roads	school	store	subdivision

PREPARATION

- Clear an area in the classroom where this project can sit for several days while the children complete it.

WHAT TO DO

1. Show the children pictures of towns and cities. Talk with the children about the various characteristics of each.
2. Tell the children they will be working together to create a model town in the classroom.
3. Show the children the materials, and invite them to explore ways to build buildings, homes, stores, and so on.
4. Consider helping the children build a basic plan for their town before proceeding.
5. As the children create buildings, help the children label them. Talk with the children about which buildings should go where, and listen as the children discuss and work through layout issues.

ASSESSMENT

To assess the children's learning, consider the following:

- Can the children build individual buildings out of the materials?
- Are the children able to work together?
- If the children are working from a plan, how closely do they follow it?

Sandie Nagel, White Lake, MI

Children's Books

Busy, Busy Town by
Richard Scarry
*In the Town All Year
'Round* by Rotraut
Susanne Berner
*My Little Shimmery
Neighborhood* by
Salina Yoon
*My Neighborhood:
Places and Faces* by Lisa
Bullard

City Ponds

4+

LEARNING OBJECTIVES

The children will:
1. Learn why many cities build ponds.
2. Learn about different kinds of ponds and their importance.
3. Improve their small motor skills.

Materials

8" x 10" or similar
    size construction
    paper
paste
child-safe scissors
colored markers
    and crayons
old nature
    magazines with
    pictures of ponds
stapler (adult use
    only)

VOCABULARY

boating	city	ducks	fish
garden	ponds	water	

PREPARATION

- Cut pictures from old magazines of ponds, city ponds, and walkways, and set out additional magazines for the children to do their own cutting.
- Fold several sheets of construction paper in half. Staple three sheets of paper at the fold to make a book. Prepare one book for each child.

WHAT TO DO

1. Gather the children together and discuss a pond they have seen. Ask what kinds of animals they have seen at ponds, and if they have ever seen a pond in a city. Talk about why we might want a pond in a city.
2. Ask the children which is larger, a pond or a lake. Talk with the children about how some ponds are natural and some are made by people.
3. Show the children the simple prepared books, as well as the markers, crayons, and magazines with pictures of ponds. Invite the children to cut out pictures and glue them in their books, or to draw pictures of ponds in cities. Talk with the children about their pond books as they work.

ASSESSMENT

To assess the children's learning, consider the following:
- Can the children describe differences between ponds and lakes?
- What are the children saying about ponds as they make their pond books?
- Are the children able to cut out pictures of ponds with minimal help?

Children's Books

Around the Pond: Who's Been Here? by Lindsay Barrett George
In the Small, Small Pond by Denise Fleming
Pond by Donald Silver and Patricia Wynne
What's in the Pond? by Anne Hunter

Shirley Anne Ramaley, Sun City, AZ

Restaurant Poster

LEARNING OBJECTIVES

The children will:
1. Learn about restaurants and the variety of cultures they represent.
2. Work cooperatively on a classroom poster.
3. Improve their oral language skills.
4. Develop their small motor skills.

Materials

poster board
picture of people
    sitting in a
    restaurant
collection of
    restaurant-related
    pictures, at least
    1 per child
glue sticks

VOCABULARY

booster chair	centerpiece	chef	food	menu
napkin	patron	restaurant	table	
tablecloth	tray	waiter	waitress	

PREPARATION

- On card stock or poster board, write the question, "What do we find at a restaurant?" in a horizontal box. Center a picture of people sitting in a restaurant under the question.

WHAT TO DO

1. Talk about different cultures and the variety of foods and restaurants found in cities.
2. Ask the children which foods and types of restaurants they prefer.
3. Show the collection of restaurant-related pictures to the children. Invite each child to select one picture.
4. Ask the children to think of a name for the restaurant in the picture and tell why they chose that name.
5. Invite the children to take turns gluing their restaurant pictures onto the poster.
6. When the final picture is in place, display the completed poster on the wall to decorate the classroom.

ASSESSMENT

To assess the children's learning, consider the following:
- Can the children discuss their experiences in restaurants and name the items in the pictures?
- Are the children able to glue their pictures of restaurants to the poster without help?

Jackie Wright, Enid, OK

Children's Books

Eating Out by Helen Oxenbury
Froggy Eats Out by Jonathan London
Going to a Restaurant by Melinda Beth Radabaugh
The Restaurant of Many Orders by Kenji Miyazawa

What Does a Jeweler Do?

LEARNING OBJECTIVES

The children will:
1. Make necklaces or bracelets.
2. Develop small motor skills.
3. Explore pattern-making.

Materials

beads in a variety
  of colors and
  styles
elastic string
scissors (adult use
  only)

VOCABULARY

bead   bracelet   jeweler   jewelry   necklace   string

PREPARATION

- Cut the string into 24" lengths for necklaces, and 7" lengths for bracelets.
- Place the string pieces and beads in the small motor center.
- Make a few pieces of jewelry to wear during the introduction of this activity, to help interest the children.

WHAT TO DO

1. Begin by showing the children the homemade jewelry you are wearing. Ask the children if people in their families also wear jewelry. Ask the children if they know where their family members got the jewelry.
2. Explain that a jeweler is someone who makes and repairs jewelry. Jewelers can work at jewelry stores, or they can make and sell jewelry at neighborhood craft fairs.
3. Set out the jewelry-making materials, and invite the children to try make necklaces and bracelets. Show the children how to string their beads on their elastic strings. Challenge the children to make ABAB and other patterns with the beads.
4. Once the children finish stringing their beads, help them tie the ends of their strings together so they can enjoy wearing their creations.

POEM

My Necklace by Laura Wynkoop

I made myself a necklace.   *It's very, very special*
It's blue just like the sea.   *Because it's just for me!*

Children's Books

Beads by Judy Ann
Sadler
The Silver Locket by
Katharine Holabird
A String of Beads by
Margarette S. Reid

ASSESSMENT

To assess the children's learning, consider the following:
- Do the children know where jewelry comes from, and can they say who makes jewelry?
- Are the children able to string beads to make necklaces or bracelets?
- Can the children make ABAB and other patterns with the beads?

Laura Wynkoop, San Dimas, CA

Fire Truck Snack

4+

LEARNING OBJECTIVES

The children will:
1. Learn about fire safety.
2. Explore the world of firefighters, fire trucks, and their purpose in the community.

Materials

paper plate
graham crackers
   (1 1/2 per truck)
mini-Oreo cookies
   (wheels)
red frosting
little pretzel sticks
black licorice
cherry

VOCABULARY

fire   fire safety   fire station   fire trucks   firefighters

PREPARATION

- Mix red food coloring into white frosting.
- Call a local fire station and ask if an officer can either visit your school for a fire safety program, or plan a field trip to the fire station.

WHAT TO DO

1. Engage the children in a discussion about fire safety.
2. Tell the children there will be a visitor from the fire department coming to meet the class. Explain the importance of the fire department to the community.
3. Before the officer from the fire department comes, work with the children to build edible fire trucks.
   - Place a whole graham cracker on a plate. With a spoon, spread frosting on one side.
   - Put half a graham cracker on top of half of the frosted cracker.
   - Dab frosting on top of the cab. Add a cherry for the light.
   - Dab frosting and add mini-Oreo cookies for wheels.
   - On the back of the truck, place two pretzels parallel to each other. Break pretzels and use frosting to stick several smaller pretzels in place to make ladder rungs.
   - Stick a black licorice stick beside the ladder for a fire hose.

ASSESSMENT

To assess the children's learning, consider the following:
- Do the children know what to do in case of a fire?
- Can the children explain what purpose the fire department serves?

Christine Kohler, Ballinger, TX

Children's Books

Big Frank's Fire Truck by Leslie McGuire
Even Firefighters Hug Their Moms by Christine Kole MacLean
Firefighters A to Z by Chris Demarist
Flashing Fire Engines by Tony Mitton

Food from Around the World

4+

Materials

food samples from
   various countries
poster board
marker
stickers or self-
   adhesive notes

LEARNING OBJECTIVES

The children will:
1. Learn about different foods from around the world.
2. Explore various cultures.

VOCABULARY

country names	cuisine	eat
food names	potluck	taste

PREPARATION

● Send out an invitation to each of the families and invite them to a classroom potluck from around the world.
● Assign each family a country to bring a food from and then let the family decide what to bring for a potluck. Offer recipes if needed.
● Set out flags and maps of the various countries from which the children's families are bringing food.

WHAT TO DO

1. Talk with the children about how different countries have distinct cuisines. Ask the children if they have ever eaten Mexican food, Ethiopian food, Italian food, Chinese food, and so on. Discuss these foods with the children.
2. When the children's families arrive with the food, direct them to their specific locations, and invite the children to sample the different types of foods.
3. Listen to the children describe and react to the foods. Write down their reactions, and after the children all sample the food, gather them together to talk about what they ate.
4. Set up a simple chart with the names of the countries and the food. Give the children stickers, and invite them to put their stickers on the section of the chart with the food they tasted.
5. With the children, look at the chart and discuss which country's food has the largest number of stickers.

ASSESSMENT

To assess the children's learning, consider the following:
● Can the children say the names of the foods they sampled and the countries those foods come from?
● Can the children look at the chart and determine which food was the one that the most children tasted?

Holly Dzierzanowski, Brenham, TX

Children's Books

Eating by Gwenyth Swain
Eating the Alphabet by Lois Elhert
Eating the Plates by Lucille Recht Penner
Showdown at the Food Pyramid by Rex Barron

Good Tooth Food

4+

LEARNING OBJECTIVES

The children will:
1. Learn about the important roles that dentists play in the community.
2. Begin to identify foods that are healthy for their teeth.

Materials

crayons or markers
magazines
newspaper
glue
paper plates

VOCABULARY

apple	carrot	celery	dentist
healthy	soda	sugar	tooth

WHAT TO DO

1. Ask the children if they have ever been to the dentist. Engage the children in a discussion about what role the dentist plays in the community.
2. Ask the children if their dentists have encouraged them to eat specific foods and to avoid other foods.
3. Make a list with two columns. Label the first column, "Food my dentist recommends" and the second column, "Food my dentist does not recommend." Put the foods the children name in one of the two columns.
4. Put the list up on the wall in the classroom for the children and their families to see.
5. Later in the week, bring in some foods from the "foods my dentist recommends" column. Ask the children to identify these foods, and say whether they are good or bad for their teeth.
6. Provide samples of the food for the children to enjoy as a snack.

TEACHER-TO-TEACHER TIP

- Collect pictures of other animals that have teeth, such as horses, snakes, dogs, sharks, cats, guinea pigs, ferrets, rabbits, chinchillas, and walruses. You may want to compare their teeth to ours and to other animals' teeth. Why are they different from each other? (Different diets)

ASSESSMENT

To assess the children's learning, consider the following:
- Do the children understand what role the dentist plays in the community?
- Can the children say if a dentist would recommend a particular food?

Children's Books

Andrew's Loose Tooth by Robert Munsch
The Berenstain Bears Visit the Dentist by Stan Berenstain
Franklin and the Tooth Fairy by Paulette Bourgeois & Brenda Clark
No Tooth, No Quarter by Jan Buller & Susan Schade
The Tooth Book by Dr. Seuss

Cookie Zingarelli, Columbus, Ohio

Being Friendly

3+

LEARNING OBJECTIVES

The children will:
1. Learn the value of being friendly.
2. Learn ways to show friendliness.

Materials

Do You Want to Be My Friend? by Eric Carle

VOCABULARY

excuse me	friendly	greeting	hello
neighbor	polite	thank you	wave

WHAT TO DO

1. As the children gather around for this activity, smile and wave at them. Ask if they need some help putting things away, and help them if they accept your offer.

2. After the children sit down, discuss what a "greeting" is and how it shows that you are friendly. Waving to people and giving them a greeting started a long time ago. When people met, they would raise their hands in greeting to show that there was nothing in their hand that would harm anyone else, so it meant they were friendly.

3. Discuss different ways to be friendly or kind to others, such as asking to help out, comforting someone who is hurt or sick, or using good manners by saying "please," "thank you," and "excuse me." Discuss why it is better to be friendly instead of being selfish or wanting things to be your own way all the time.

4. Read Eric Carle's *Do You Want to Be My Friend?* with the children, noting greetings and acts of friendliness or kindness.

TEACHER-TO-TEACHER TIP

- Consider including a short lesson on being careful as well as friendly. Tell the children that most grown-ups are good and kind, but not to get into a car with someone they do not know or have an uncomfortable feeling about. If they get a funny feeling that something is just not right, they should tell an adult they trust.

ASSESSMENT

To assess the children's learning, consider the following:
- Do the children wave to others, such as the janitor or other teachers or children not in their own classroom?
- Do the children show kindness by helping others and by using good manners?

Kay Flowers, Summerfield, OH

Children's Books

Friends by Helme Heine
How to Lose All Your Friends by Nancy L. Carlson
In My Neighborhood by Mari C. Schuh
My Street by Rebecca Treays

Many Ways to Say Hello 3+

LEARNING OBJECTIVES

The children will:
1. Learn that there are many languages in the world.
2. Recognize that different cultures have different ways of saying "hello."
3. Accept differences, and celebrate the world's diversity.

Materials

markers
construction paper
several translations
   of how to say
   "hello"
globe or world map

VOCABULARY

country	friendly	greeting	hello
home	language	polite	

PREPARATION

- Prepare "hello" signs in the different languages that your children speak and other languages that are easy to say and remember. Remember to write the name of the language on the sign as well. Make one sign per child.
- Here are some examples of how to say "hello" in foreign languages:
  Chinese: Nihao ("nee-how")
  French: Bonjour ("bohn-zhoor")
  Hawai'ian: Aloha
  Italian: Ciao ("chow")
  Spanish: Hola ("oh-lah")

WHAT TO DO

1. As the children arrive in the morning, give each child one of the translated "hello" signs.
2. Explain to each child that the signs say "hello" in different languages. Help the children pronounce the "hello" on the signs they are holding.
3. After all the children arrive, pair the children and have each pair hold their signs up to one another and practice saying "hello" in the languages on their partners' signs. Encourage the children to help one another with the pronunciation.
4. After a little while, have the children form new pairs.
5. Show the children the world map or globe, and point out and describe the countries that speak the languages they have been speaking.

ASSESSMENT

To assess the children's learning, consider the following:
- Can the children say "hello" in the languages on their signs?
- Can the children name the languages in which they are saying "hello"?
- Are the children able to help one another say "hello" in different languages?

Children's Books

Cock-a Doodle Doo! What Does it Sound Like to You? by Marc Robinson
Greetings, Asia! by April Pulley Sayre
Hello, Red Fox by Eric Carle
Jambo Means Hello by Muriel L. Feelings
What Is Your Language? by Debra Leventhal

Eileen Lucas, Fort McMurray, Alberta, Canada

Recycle at Home and in the City

LEARNING OBJECTIVES

The children will:
1. Learn how and what to recycle.
2. Learn how to sort and classify objects.
3. Improve their large motor skills.

Materials

book about recycling
4 large plastic containers or bins
variety of child-safe and clean recyclable and non-recyclable objects

VOCABULARY

city   clean   home   recycle   trash

PREPARATION

- Set up the containers next to each other. Set the other materials nearby and not in any certain order. On one container, write "Cans" in large black letters. On another container, write "Plastic." On the third, write "Paper." On the last container, write "No Recycle."

WHAT TO DO

1. Read the children a book about recycling (see list to the left for suggestions) and then talk with the children about recycling. Ask the children if they have ever recycled materials. Ask if their families have different containers to separate trash and recycling. Talk about the importance of recycling for the community.

2. Talk with the children about how to know what to recycle. Show the children recyclable and non-recyclable objects.

3. One by one, invite each child to pick out an object and decide if it is recyclable or not, and then put it into the appropriate bin.

Children's Books

The Adventures of a Plastic Bottle: A Story About Recycling by Alison Inches and Pete Whitehead
The Adventures of an Aluminum Can: A Story About Recycling by Alison Inches and Mark Chambers
The Three Rs: Reuse, Reduce, Recycle by Nuria Roca and Rosa Curto

ASSESSMENT

To assess the children's learning, consider the following:
- Can the children describe why recycling is important?
- Can the children put materials in the correct bins?

Shirley Anne Ramaley, Sun City, AZ

Talking with the Neighbors 4+

The children will:

1. Develop their social skills.
2. Role play.
3. Develop their self-confidence.
4. Enhance their large motor skills.

Materials

2 rakes
2 snow shovels
crumpled white tissue paper (to represent snow)
crumpled tissue paper balls in orange red, brown and yellow, to represent leaves
masking tape

VOCABULARY

ask	kind	listen	neighbor
question	talk	yard	

PREPARATION

- Use masking tape to mark off four "pieces of property," each about 2' x 3'.
- Sprinkle the leaves randomly around two adjoining "properties."
- Sprinkle the snow randomly around two adjoining "properties."

WHAT TO DO

1. Invite the children to name some of the people in their neighborhoods.
2. Ask the children to think of ways they can show kindness to their neighbors.
3. Explain that one way to show kindness to neighbors is to visit with them when they are outside working. Children can ask questions such as, "How are you?," "How is your job going?," "What has your family been doing lately?," "Do you need any help?," and "Do you have any plans for a vacation?"
4. Select three children from the class and have them demonstrate how to use the shovels to shovel the "snow" and the rakes to "rake the leaves" into piles on imaginary properties.
5. Invite the children to use the yard tools as they pretend to be raking and shoveling, and to talk with one another as though they were friendly neighbors.

ASSESSMENT

To assess the children's learning, consider the following:

- What kinds of questions do the children ask one another when pretending to be neighbors?
- Are the children able to rake and shovel the "leaves" and "snow"?
- Can the children describe ways to be kind to their neighbors?

Mary J. Murray, Mazomanie, WI

Children's Books

Around Our Way on Neighbor's Day by Tameka Fryer Brown
The Berenstain Bears Love Their Neighbors by Jan and Stan Berenstain
Bobo and the New Neighbor by Gail Page
New Dog Next Door by Elizabeth Bridgman

Make a Classroom Book 4+

LEARNING OBJECTIVES

The children will:
1. Learn to identify various community jobs.
2. Recognize themselves as members of the classroom community.
3. Associate written words with statements made by classmates.

Materials

camera
dress-up clothes
    and props of
    community
    helpers
images of
    community
    helpers
construction paper
glue or rubber
    cement (adult
    use only)
marker
stapler (adult use
    only)

VOCABULARY

community	doctor	firefighter	jobs	librarian
mail carrier	neighborhood	police officer	sanitation worker	

WHAT TO DO

1. Talk with the children about what they want to be when they grow up. Point out that there are many people in the community who help the children. Show the children the pictures of community helpers. Ask the children which helpers they have met.
2. Show the children the various dress-up clothes and props, and invite the children to put on the clothes that match the careers they want to explore. Take pictures of the children in their career clothes.
3. Print out the pictures of the children, paste them onto pieces of construction paper, and help the children write a note at the bottom of their pictures, explaining why they like the community helpers they dressed as. Invite the children to draw around their pictures as well.
4. Gather all the children's pictures together and staple them into a book. Add a cover page and title it "Our Classroom Careers," or something similar. Place the book in the class library for the children to explore.

ASSESSMENT

To assess the children's learning, consider the following:
● Can the children name the various community helpers in the pictures?
● Which community helpers do each of the children like best?

Tammy Utchek Lee, Bloomingdale, IL

Children's Books

Career Day by Anne
    Rockwell
Jobs People Do by
    Felicity Brooks
Sally Gets a Job by
    Stephen Huneck
When I Grow Up by
    P.K. Hallinan

Three Countries of North America

5+

Materials

large map of North America

world globe (if available)

outline drawing of North America's countries on 8" x 10" paper

Children's Books

Discovering Geography of North America with Books Kids Love by Carol J. Fuhler and Audra Loyal

North America by Alan Fowler

North America by David Petersen

North America by Cheryl Striveildi

Welcome to North America by April Pulley Sayre

LEARNING OBJECTIVES

The children will:

1. Explore maps and globes.
2. Develop an awareness of North America.
3. Develop their vocabularies.

VOCABULARY

border	Canada	continent	country	globe
map	Mexico	North America	United States	world

PREPARATION

● If necessary, send a note home with the children asking parents to lend a globe to the classroom for this activity.

WHAT TO DO

1. Set out the map and globe.
2. Talk with the children about the continent of North America. Show the children the map of North America and challenge them to find the United States, Mexico, and Canada.
3. Read the children a book about the countries in North America (see the list to the left for suggestions).
4. Provide the children with markers, crayons, and colored pencils. Invite the children to draw pictures about the countries in North America.

TEACHER-TOTEACHER TIP

● If a child has a family member who was born and raised in Canada or Mexico, ask if that person will attend class and talk with the children about their experiences. Encourage the children to ask questions.

ASSESSMENT

To assess the children's learning, consider the following:

● Can the children identify the United States on a map of North America?
● Can the children name the other countries in North America?
● How well can the children draw the countries in North America?

Shirley Anne Ramaley, Sun City, AZ

When I Grow Up I Want to Be...

5+

LEARNING OBJECTIVES

The children will:
1. Familiarize themselves with the duties of various professions.
2. Develop their small motor skills.

Materials

copier paper
markers and
    crayons
pictures of workers
child-safe scissors
glue sticks
images of various
    professions

VOCABULARY

adult   career   grow up   job
occupation   responsibility   vocation   work

WHAT TO DO

1. Read stories to the children and talk about things that people do when they go to work.
2. Hold up pictures and see if any of the children recognize some of the people in various jobs. For example, show the children a picture of a trash truck, a picture of a mail carrier, and so on.
3. Tell the children that they are going to make their own book about things that they want to be when they grow up.
4. Give each child a turn describing what he wants to be when he grows up. Write down the information on a sheet of paper, and have the children illustrate their pages. Also provide children with pictures and scissors and invite the children to cut out and glue the pictures of the professions they want to explore on their pages.
5. When all the children finish illustrating their pages, laminate and bind them together. Read the book to the children.
6. Let each child have a turn taking the book home.

ASSESSMENT

To assess the children's learning, consider the following:
● Can the children identify the various professions shown in the pictures?
● Can the children describe the duties of the professions they want to have when they grow up?
● Were the children able to illustrate their pages of the book?

Holly Dzierzanowski, Brenham, TX

Children's Books

ABC of Jobs People Do by Roger Priddy
Career Day by Anne Rockwell
Clifford Gets a Job by Norman Birdwell
Jobs by Angela Lambert
What Will I Be? by James Levin

Index of Children's Books

Index